GIRL ON A WIRE

GIRL ON A WIRE

Walking the Line Between Faith and Freedom
in the Westboro Baptist Church

LIBBY PHELPS

with Sara Stewart

Skyhorse Publishing

Skyhorse Publishing books may be purchased in bulk at special discounts for sales promotion, corporate gifts, fund-raising, or educational purposes. Special editions can also be created to specifications. For details, contact the Special Sales Department, Skyhorse Publishing, 307 West 36th Street, 11th Floor, New York, NY 10018 or info@skyhorsepublishing.com.

Skyhorse® and Skyhorse Publishing® are registered trademarks of Skyhorse Publishing, Inc.®, a Delaware corporation.

Visit our website at www.skyhorsepublishing.com.

10 9 8 7 6 5 4 3 2 1

Library of Congress Cataloging-in-Publication Data is available on file.

Cover design by Erin Seaward-Hiatt

Print ISBN: 978-1-5107-0325-4
Ebook ISBN: 978-1-5107-0327-8

Printed in the United States of America

For My Loved Ones

GIRL ON A WIRE

Chapter One

THE WESTBORO BAPTIST CHURCH

It was a hot, sunny summer morning in Topeka, and I'd settled myself beside the swimming pool to write. Stretched out on a lounge chair, clad in a T-shirt and running shorts, I scribbled intently in my pink journal with my favorite turquoise ballpoint pen. My grandfather walked laps around the running track that encircled the pool, wearing a nylon sweatsuit despite the heat. He wasn't allowed to actually run anymore because it was bad for his elderly hips and knees, but he still got out there every day, striding around. A man on a mission.

Taking a break to sip from his water bottle, Gramps strolled across the lawn to my chair and peered over my shoulder.

"What you working on, Lib?" he asked with a grin. I angled the book up so he could see my list of the torments of hell, outlined in my looping handwriting.

Miraculously, I had been born a member of the only church on Earth whose congregation was going to heaven, and I had been taught from birth what happened to everyone who wasn't. Or, for that matter, to anyone in our family who strayed from the path of righteousness.

A type-A student both in school and in church, I wanted to make sure I knew all of God's punishments by heart. You should know them too, because that's where my church says you're headed.

You're doomed to eternal torment in the fires of hell, as I wrote in that notebook, where the worm that eats on you never dies, where flames will ceaselessly shoot out of your eyeballs. Where you will look at others around you, amazed and disbelieving that you are all actually there, writhing in this agonizing and never-ending suffering. Where your pain threshold incrementally increases as your pain tolerance increases. Where there is a great gulf between you and the people in heaven, who can see you being tortured and taunt you for not heeding their warnings about God's wrath while you were alive.

Gramps's blue eyes skimmed my itemized list of everlasting damnation, each item bullet-pointed with a different metallic color, and his face lit up into a bigger smile. Bending his tall frame down, he kissed me gently on the forehead.

"I love you," he told me. "I love you, I love you." He walked away and resumed his exercise. Staring down at the list, my eyes filled with tears in spite of myself. Gramps loved me best when I was terrified for my immortal soul—which was most of the time.

My late grandfather, Fred Phelps, was the founder of the Westboro Baptist Church. The church is made up of about seventy people, and 90 percent of them are members of my immediate or extended family. (A few other families would join over the years, but I was always skeptical of them.)

The Phelps clan is the backbone of the WBC. For a man who lived nearly his entire life in a small Kansan town, Gramps's name and face are well known all around the world. When people speak of him, the word "hate" comes up a lot. As in, "hate group." Or "the most hated man in America." Or "the man who loves to hate," as one news story put it. The media covered my grandfather endlessly, which he loved. Did it bother him that they almost uniformly wrote about how terrible he was? Quite the opposite. He saw himself as a prophet, and as he often told us, throughout history people have always scorned prophets—right up until their prophecies come true.

As a member of his flock and family, I was more than just sheltered—I was actively warned against the corruption of the outside world. Again and again, in sermons and private conversations, I was told that civilization outside of WBC was made up of sinners, alcoholics, drug addicts, and lost souls with no moral compass. There was no gray area: You were either one of us, or you were depraved and doomed. So I was terrified of what lurked beyond the protective walls my family had carefully erected around me—terrified especially of gay people, because according to the WBC, homosexuals were the absolute worst of the worst, the most dangerous group of people in the world. As long as I can remember, I was told daily that they were the bottom rung on the ladder of depravity, sending all of America to hell in a "faggot's handbasket." Gays were to blame for all the country's natural disasters, terrorist attacks, and school shootings. My only view of life outside

WBC was that it was an orgy of sin, that absolutely everyone was bound for eternal damnation. This was what I was taught, and believed, for the first twenty-five years of my life. I thought I was one of the few people God had selected to be His own. I felt privileged that by the grace of God I was born into this family, and I believed I was handpicked to represent God on the mean streets of America. Like all the other members of my family (excepting those who had made the foolish decision to leave the church), I was thankful to have been chosen out of this corrupt and sinful generation, while all others were blinded by the truth.

WBC is best known for our picketing, which began in earnest in the early 1990s. We picketed pop concerts, football games, churches of every denomination, and—most notoriously—the funerals of American soldiers and victims of hate crimes. You know who we are. You've gasped at television footage of me and my family at memorial services for American soldiers, waving signs that say THANK GOD FOR DEAD SOLDIERS. You have seen the images, each colorful neon sign emblazoned with a hateful, shocking slogan: GOD: USA's TERRORIST. GOD HATES JEWS. THANK GOD FOR 9/11. The international media have covered our protests with unflagging interest, to the deep satisfaction of the WBC leaders.

For over twenty years, the church has picketed every day, 365 days a year. No exceptions. There is at least one daily picket in Topeka, our hometown, and sometimes there is also an organized picket in another city. GOD HATES FAGS, our most well-known sign, was the enduring mantra of the church.

Gramps's focus on gays came from the Biblical verse Leviticus 18:22: "Thou shalt not lie with mankind, as with womankind: it is abomination." Twelve simple words, Gramps would always say. However, the homosexual population only really became the church's crusade after Gramps's complaints—about a park in our town being used as a hookup spot for gay men—were ignored. Rather than heeding his warnings about it, prominent people in town and fellow churches deemed his quest to have the park "cleaned up" extremist and homophobic. Their disdain inspired my grandfather to begin what he saw as his holy mission of calling out the unrepentant depravity of Topeka's residents—and eventually the entire world.

When the picketing first began, WBC specifically targeted the gay population at pride parades and LGBT-friendly organizations or places that employed people known to be openly gay. Then we branched out to fallen soldiers' funerals—a 180-degree reversal of Gramps's previous attitude toward the military, up until the late '90s, when he would pray for US soldiers in sermons, referring to them as "our boys." Once Gramps decided the United States as a whole was on a fast track straight to hell, he proclaimed that no one should be fighting for a nation that supports and enables homosexuality. "A nation is doomed when it proudly embraces, exalts, and institutionalizes fag filth," Gramps told us again and again in sermons and during pickets. Americans were "worshipping dead soldiers," he told us. Instead of paying tribute to the dead body, he would explain to us, people should be warning their fellow man of the dangers of going to hell like the fallen soldier. God killed that soldier, he said, for fighting for a "filthy fag nation, a sinful nation given over to perversion, a rebellious nation who will not hear the Word of the Lord, a nation covered with wounds and bruises and putrefying sores from the sole of her foot to the top of her woolly head." (Why the nation had a woolly head, I was never quite sure.)

More specifically, Gramps preached to us that God was killing soldiers because Americans bombed us on August 20,

1995, when a small improvised explosive device went off outside my Aunt Shirley's house, destroying property (but thankfully not injuring any of us). The church sent out a flyer offering a reward of several thousand dollars, and we eventually found out a local Washburn University student did it. He was found guilty and sentenced to only a couple of weeks in jail, which didn't surprise my family members—they already thought everyone was out to get them, and that the government was in on it too. In retaliatory wrath, Gramps preached, God was killing Americans. "For it is written, Vengeance is mine; I will repay, saith the Lord," he quoted from Romans 12:19.

PEOPLE OFTEN ASK ME ABOUT THE MOTIVES BEHIND WBC's public face. Do they really believe all of this shock-tactic stuff? Is it a publicity stunt? Are they doing it simply to be cruel? The bottom line is that WBC members absolutely believe in what they're saying. They are convinced they're doing the right thing—that this is the best way to love their neighbor. Sparing someone's feelings doesn't enter into the equation. We were taught that a true believer shows love by obeying God and urges their neighbor to do the same, and that to love thy neighbor is to rebuke him or her. WBC sees pickets as a battlefield: God's people vs. "workers of iniquity," or those who persecute the elect (that is to say, us). The elect were chosen "before the foundation of the world," as the Bible says in Ephesians 1:4, so Westboro members were predestined as righteous prophets. The words on our signs—and coming from the picketers' mouths—are really intended more for overall shock value than to make anyone feel bad, although we were often confronted with people brought to tears by our placards. Their visible pain was entirely beside the point, in the church's view.

Short sound bites grab people's attention and spark interest, as we were taught early and often in church and in picketing meetings. As a result, passersby will look at the signs and have to make a choice: to serve God by picketing with us, or to turn their backs (which would be like turning their backs on God) and continue to be part of unholy America.

We were told every day that the world would loathe us for our religious beliefs, and that the world's hatred would make us stronger. If people hate you, we were taught, you're doing it right. There's a verse in the Bible that says, "Cry aloud, spare not, lift up thy voice like a trumpet, and shew my people their transgression." From the time I was born, I was taught that hating sinners and telling them so made me a good person. It made our "calling and election sure," as the Bible says in 2 Peter 1:10. We were told to wear our persecution like a badge of honor. It was, after all, a small price to pay for our endless days in heaven, when we would be able to watch all the sinners roasting below us in hell while we enjoyed the bounty of eternal life. We would always say nonchalantly, "Sorry, you're going to hell and there's nothing you can do about it."

But being part of God's elect didn't make us immune from the terror of damnation. If one of us ever screwed up, our family members would immediately warn us that we'd be headed to the same place if we didn't straighten up right quick. My relatives would tell me they loved me in the same breath as they'd tell me exactly what would happen to me if I strayed from the path of church-approved righteousness. My grandfather's love for his family and his belief in his ministry were deeply intertwined. Since before I could walk or talk, the church and its teachings were the centerpiece of my life. Growing up, I heard the term "filthy fags" a lot more often than I heard the phrase "I love you." Gramps taught us that to love each other, and our family, meant for us to tell everyone God hates them—and that everyone else, in turn, hated us for telling them our righteous beliefs. It was a vicious cycle.

When I was growing up, people would often remark that the Phelps children were so well behaved. Well, of course we were, because we didn't ever want to disappoint anyone and lose our place in heaven. We kids would have conversations among ourselves about how terrifying it all was. We always wanted to get it right, so we wouldn't be consigned to the flames of hell forever. When I had thoughts that I was doing the wrong thing, I attributed it to the devil and almost instantly pushed those thoughts aside.

Since I was born into this belief system, most of what I did growing up felt pretty normal. I won't tell you here that I doubted the teachings of the church all along, because I didn't—at least, not very often. I learned from a young age to push any "bad" thoughts to the back of my mind, as if those thoughts had never existed. I also learned early on that negative thoughts or doubts were not to be discussed openly for fear of public humiliation within the confines of the church. But every so often, they'd come to mind full force, like on 9/11. My initial reaction was pure and utter shock, while the elder church member's reaction was to joyfully dance in celebration—or to "dance a little jig," as they frequently called it.

Most of the world saw Gramps as a condemning, hateful, firebrand cult leader—a man who would be impossible to like, let alone love—but the truth is that to me, he was a real grandfather as well as an all-consuming spiritual leader. When he wasn't talking religion, he seemed like a typical Southern gentleman. He had impeccable manners, and insisted on looking his Sunday best every day, with his shoes shined and clothes pressed.

Gramps always made me feel like I held a special place in his heart. It wasn't that he never got irritated with me—he did have a quick and fiery temper, which could be much scarier one-on-one than hearing him preaching in church or sermonizing at a picket. His booming voice, when directed at us, could be like the angry voice of God Himself. Somehow, though, I seemed to be exempt from most of Gramps's ire. He didn't reproach me nearly as much as he did my cousins and sisters. And when he did get upset with me, I could tell he felt bad for hurting my feelings, and he would usually try to make up for it in some small way. We were close, and I really loved him.

Born in 1929 in Meridian, Mississippi, my grandfather was a dedicated Boy Scout who went on to receive the prestigious Eagle Scout award. At age seventeen, he received a principal appointment to West Point Military Academy; shortly after, he turned it down because of his young age and in order to pursue the ministry, becoming an ordained minister on September 8, 1947, at the hands of a Southern Baptist preacher. He met his wife, Margie Simms—Gran, to us—in Phoenix at the Arizona Bible Institute in October 1951. They were married in 1952, in Glendale, Arizona. Gramps and Gran had thirteen children. My dad, Fred Phelps Jr., is the eldest. Four of my dad's siblings have left the church. The most influential ones still in the group are my uncle Tim, my aunt Margie Phelps, and my aunt Shirley Phelps-Roper.

Gramps and Gran moved to Topeka in May of 1954 with my dad. The first-ever church service at their spacious, mid-century home—which still houses the WBC chapel—was held in November 1955, and from then on it hosted Sunday services nearly every week and continues to this day. But for many years before the picketing started, my grandfather ran a more traditional ministry. Before he opened his own church, he was an associate pastor at Topeka's East Side Baptist Church. He split off to create its affiliate, the Westboro Baptist Church, eventually severing all ties with East Side. WBC is what is known as nondenominational, but Gramps would refer to it as "old-school, primitive Baptist," since its members don't share many views with other religious groups, including other Baptists. With very few exceptions, there was never any other congregation Gramps deemed as righteous as ours.

Gramps would often explain to us with genuine regret that although no one preached the Bible like he did, there was a time when all preachers would do it. John Calvin's Five Points of Calvinism—total depravity, unconditional election, limited atonement, irresistible grace, and perseverance of the saints, often shortened to their acronym "TULIP"—were considered the building blocks of Christianity by many preachers of my grandfather's generation. These same people were inspired by the famous sermon "Sinners in the Hands of an Angry God," delivered by Puritan preacher and theologian Jonathan Edwards in 1741. As the title implies, Edwards did not believe in a God who forgives everyone; in his sermon, he enumerates the many ways one might end up condemned to burn in hell. Over time, old-school preachers like Edwards were replaced by modern thinkers who believe in what Gramps would call "the great Arminian lie," after sixteenth-century Protestant preacher Jacobus Arminius: the idea that God loves everyone.

Early on, my grandfather realized it would be helpful to his ministry to have a law degree as well. He graduated from Washburn University Law School in Topeka in 1964, founding the Phelps-Chartered law firm soon afterward. He was a well-known lawyer in town for years, famed for his passionate defenses in civil rights cases. He was said to be a "brilliant" civil rights attorney (including in a CNN story about him) and would take on racial discrimination cases no one else would touch at that time. He represented the likes of Gale Sayers, a professional football player who contacted Gramps when he played college ball at the University of Kansas. I met Gale years later at a book signing; I told him who I was and he leaned in close to me and whispered, "Tell your grandfather 'hi' for me." I could tell he was nervous saying this; it seemed he was proud and appreciative of what Gramps had done for the civil rights movement, but understandably didn't want to be associated with his anti-gay crusade. Gramps also re-opened the prominent *Brown v. Board of Education* in a suit that maintained the Kansas school system hadn't fully implemented the dismantling of "separate but equal" schools as it had been ordered to do in the Supreme Court ruling of 1954. For decades after the church's founding, Gramps worked as a civil rights lawyer during the week, and an old-school preacher on Sundays. He even received an award from the NAACP for his work on behalf of black clients.

Later, Gramps would actually use his background in civil rights to shore up his conviction that gay people didn't deserve equal rights. Since he believed that being gay was a choice—unlike race—he had no problem separating his anti-gay rhetoric from his past as a defender of victims of racial discrimination.

Gramps stopped his civil rights work when he was disbarred in Kansas in 1979, after a case in which he sued a court clerk who failed to provide materials for his case and was accused of cross-examining her too abusively, or "witness badgering." The court wrote at the time: "The seriousness of the present case coupled with his previous record leads this court to the conclusion that respondent has little regard for the ethics of his profession." That was the official position, although our family always believed their conclusion may have been made because of his standing up for blacks in a time and place where it wasn't entirely accepted. In 1989 he agreed to stop practicing federal law as well. From then on, he focused on the ministry, but insisted his children get law degrees so they could continue the family business. This turned out to be a key element of the church's ongoing battle against those who would try to shut them down for protesting. Having a family full of lawyers who knew free-speech legal history backward and forward meant we were almost certain to win any legal action brought against us, as we would most memorably demonstrate in the Albert Snyder Supreme Court case in 2011, when my aunts Margie and Shirley mounted their own defense of the WBC and won.

As far back as I can remember, our church has consisted of three families: the Phelpses, who make up the vast majority of members; the Hockenbarger family; and the Davis family. In the summer of 2001, the Drain family moved to Topeka to join the church; their daughter, Lauren, was kicked out of the church a few years after they arrived, while her father Steve would go on to a position of leadership, a bizarre and unexpected turn of events. Several new members have joined WBC via marriage since my departure, but my family has always been the foundation of the church.

Although he's Gramps's firstborn, my father, Fred Jr., was never seen as a successor in terms of leading the church. Quieter, more mild-mannered, and less enamored of the spotlight, my dad has always been a devout member of the church but not a very verbal one. He avoids conflict whenever he can, and he doesn't like being in the media, though he'll consent to an interview if there's no way around it. We are often ambushed by protestors with cameras while picketing, and my aunt

Shirley firmly believes that any publicity is good publicity for us. Physically, my father doesn't look that much like my grandfather, other than their taller-than-average height. You probably wouldn't even guess they were related.

At the age of seventeen, my father left the church to attend Kansas State University, in the town of Manhattan. Many of the kids in his generation did the same, leaving for college and coming back. This makes them different from my generation; we were discouraged from ever leaving Topeka, and if we wanted to get a higher education, we were instructed to get it at our local institution, Washburn University. My dad met my mom, a music major, in college.

My mother, Betty, was from a very small Kansas town called Green, and she was a Methodist, which Gramps deemed acceptable (his approval being absolutely necessary for their getting married). They wed in 1974, and both attended law school at the insistence of my grandfather. Having followed in Gramps's footsteps, my father did much of his early work on civil right cases and in local politics.

My mom is a petite woman with long, brown (now graying) hair and brown eyes. My dad loved to tell us the story about how, when he first met her, the first thing he noticed was that "she had one big honker of a nose!" Some people think I look like her, but I don't see the strong resemblance others exclaim over. She is a kind, sweet woman who is always very submissive to my father, as the church taught wives should be. She always went along with the prevailing views of the church and never spoke up even if she disagreed. I honestly wouldn't have known if she differed from the church's positions on anything, because she would never say if she did or not—and it wasn't my place to ask. She is very proper and doesn't curse; she is so against cursing that when someone nearly hit her while she was driving me and Sara home from a picket one day, she blurted "schnike-doo!" How she came up with that word in such a stressful situation is beyond me, but is one of my favorite memories of my mom and will always make me laugh. We were very close, in our way, though she was never physically affectionate with me. I don't remember her ever kissing or hugging me until I got really sick when I was seventeen years old. (She did rub and tickle my back all the time; it was so relaxing. She did it even when she was tired—sometimes she would sigh if I asked her to, but she still did it. She was such a great mom.) I only learned later in life that this wasn't the normal way of things.

I am the youngest of four siblings. Like all the church members, my parents went by the Bible verse that says "Be fruitful and multiply," so no one was allowed to use birth control. Our numbers were small in comparison to the other families; my cousin Megan is one of eleven. My brother, Ben, is the oldest, and the creator of the church's infamous website www.godhatesfags.com. Eight years separate me from my brother. My oldest sister is Sharon; she left the church when I was about fifteen years old. My other sister is Sara. She's three years older than me, and we were very close growing up. She left the church two years ago, but we hardly ever talk now—we reacted in different ways to leaving, and sadly it caused a rift between us that I'm working on changing. Up until I left, my family was my world. None of us had close friends outside of the church. It wasn't encouraged, and we were basically told that the rest of the world hated us anyway. My cousins and sister were always my best friends—my only friends, really.

My closest companion among the cousins was Megan, who was three years younger than me and a truly intelligent, curious person. She was an independent thinker but tended to keep those thoughts to herself (or share them with only me); she had a way of avoiding speaking out against the opinion of any group she was in, a trait that served her well in the church. With her tightly curled brown hair and blue-green eyes, she always got a lot of attention from boys, like most of the Phelps girls did. This was something she and I would strategize about—going so far as to write scripts for ourselves as to how we'd respond to pickup lines from guys. She could make anyone feel comfortable around her, even journalists who were clearly trying to rile her up into a caricature of a crazy fundamentalist. My other closest friends among the cousins were Josh, Megan's older brother; Jacob, who was the son of our aunt Margie; and Jael, daughter of our uncle Jon.

THE EXTENDED PHELPS CLAN WAS CLOSE-KNIT AND, AT TIMES, terrifying to me, especially my aunt Shirley. From the time I was little, Shirley—or Shirl, as we called her—was Gramps's right-hand woman, with a seemingly endless capacity for managing several tasks at once and keeping her many children in line at the same time. She was in charge of who went to which picket, who answered media inquiries, and whom was assigned which chores. With her long, salt-and-pepper hair, crooked teeth, and beaklike nose, she always reminded me a bit of a penguin—or a wicked witch, which she would come to represent to me as I got older. Among all of us, she was the one who seemed to take the most genuine pleasure in seeing other people hurt by our pickets. When someone would get upset while talking to one of us on the picket line, she'd say something like, "See how mad the person is getting over there? Isn't that great? Their heart is getting harder as we speak." We never got along very well. She always thought

I wasn't doing enough to be helpful, and when Shirl thought we weren't doing enough, there would be an outburst. When she was really mad, she had a stare that would pierce right through us. Fear of her disapproval would regularly make my stomach hurt, sometimes until I threw up. I still get chills when I think about getting on Shirl's bad side.

Shirl's redheaded brother, Tim, was the cool uncle in the family. When we were little and had sleepovers, he would dress up as a ninja and show up to play hide and seek with us, which thrilled us every time. He was a forceful personality, always front and center helping Gramps lead church services. But as I got older, he and his wife, Lee Ann, got in trouble with Shirl and the other elders for being, as they called it, bad with money. Debt was a shameful thing to have in our family, and Tim got called before the members to account for his bad decision-making. My aunt Marge, also a redhead, was one of the quickest wits in the church. She is a good writer, and did a lot of the lyrics for our pop song parodies. A sharp lawyer, she handled most of the arguments during the Supreme Court case. She was protective of the girls, and seemed to be in our corner more than many of the grownups. I recall watching a movie when I was little where there was a naked woman in it. Her reaction was, "Boys, you close your eyes. You can't watch this. But the girls can." When I was seventeen, she took me on a special aunt-niece cruise to the Bahamas.

Nice trips were pretty regular occurrences in my life; I was in many respects a very well-cared-for kid. I was surrounded by people who were smart, hardworking, and interested in my well-being, and who could be incredibly kind when they wanted to be. My family lived in a three-story house in one of the nicest neighborhoods in Topeka, a half mile from the

WBC compound, which shares its backyard with a majority of my family members. The fact that we lived in a family compound—and were not encouraged to be friendly with anyone other than our immediate family members—didn't really worry me. After all, I was the one who was going to heaven for all of eternity, and what were earthly friends compared to that?

The shared backyard of our block had everything a kid could want: an in-ground swimming pool where I would play with my cousins and race my dad; a track around the pool as well as around a big, sprawling lawn where we would play badminton and flag football; and playground toys for the younger kids. On the other side of the church there was a basketball court and a volleyball court.

Gramps and Gran lived in the biggest house on the block, the one that was also home to the church itself. One side of the brown and white house, the one that looked out onto the road, sported a huge banner proclaiming GODHATESAMERICA. COM. A marquee outside also bore a church message, usually something along the same lines, though frequently we would discover it had been doctored with spray-paint from vandals. A black wrought iron fence connected to a taller brown lattice fence surrounded the property. The fences stayed locked and were equipped with video surveillance most of the time, as Gramps had become increasingly paranoid in his later years.

At Gramps and Gran's house, the cousins and I mostly spent time in the spacious, cork-floored kitchen helping Gran cook or clean, or listening to Gramps practicing his sermons. He would always work on his sermon all week long, and if you stopped by the house while he was doing it, he would sit you down at the table and practice on you. You were in for it then, because his sermons would take an hour or longer.

Gran would generally either be sitting next to him, cleaning the house, or watching retro shows on the TV Land channel on the small television in her room.

Gramps would sleep upstairs in the master bedroom, but for as long as I can remember, he and Gran hadn't shared a bed. She suffered from terrible kyphosis, a spinal condition that creates a hump on the back and makes it nearly impossible to lie down straight. So for the most part, she slept on a blue La-Z-Boy recliner in front of a brick fireplace in a small room downstairs, next to the kitchen. If the door to her room was opened, we could see directly through the kitchen into the sanctuary.

Ever since I was born, Sundays meant church in that sanctuary; for many years we had two services, one in the morning and one in the evening. Later, when the picketing started, there wasn't enough time for that, so we narrowed it down to one service that started at noon. There was never any separate Sunday school for the kids. Gramps thought that since there was no way to tell when a child might start understanding, he might as well start teaching the fundamentals of our religion as soon as possible. So I was brought to church services from the time I was a baby, and quickly learned not to fidget. That could earn you a slap, as I'd once seen demonstrated on my cousin Zach.

Every Sunday morning, we would file into the low-ceilinged chapel with its twenty-odd rows of pews, pulpit, organ and piano, and baptismal area. Everyone had their assigned seat there on the red-upholstered pews. For years, I sat toward the back with my parents, and then eventually I moved up to sit next to my sister Sara in the second row on the left side. Originally I moved up to replace my aunt Lizz, temporarily, but then we liked sitting there, so we kept it that way.

All the women have to wear headscarves in church to show humility before God. We would fold a scarf into a triangle and tie it over our heads. It looked oddly incongruous with the modern casual clothes we all wore—nobody really got dressed up for church, unless it was a special occasion—but this was a longtime rule and we never questioned it.

A typical church service went something like this: First, my uncle Tim would go up to the front and open the big brown book (or other WBC hymnal). Then he led us in song. Usually we'd sing something like "Ten Thousand Angels," or "How Great Thou Art," or "Faith Is the Victory," or "His Eye Is on the Sparrow." My father played the piano for the church services. He practiced every day on the piano at our house, especially on Saturday nights before the Sunday service. He was really good, and I loved falling asleep with his music being the last thing I heard.

Then Tim would say, "Now let us pray." Everyone put their head down and we'd stay silent for just a couple of minutes as either he or someone he asked gave the prayer.

After that, Gramps would come up to the pulpit for the sermon, the primary focus of the service, and the part of the service that would be recorded for the Internet. For most of my life he stood at the lectern, but in later years, as he got weaker, he would sit. No matter where he was, though, his sermons were always bombastic and angry. When standing, he would often pound the pulpit, telling us to "Wake up!" Usually he meant it as a metaphor, although every so often we might be daydreaming—and then we'd be scared that Gramps had seen our minds wandering. He seemed to see everything. But mostly he was talking to the world, not just us. In recent years, every sermon was recorded and put on our website, where anyone could watch or listen to it.

The sermons were long, and often repetitive, but Gramps was tireless as he delivered them. His topics were usually variations on the theme of damnation (of others) and salvation (of us).

Sometimes, they focused on our immediate neighbors: "Topeka, Kansas, the only place in the universe with the zip code of 666, which the Bible declares to be the mark of the beast, may be the most evil place on earth; where Satan's seat is; where the synagogue of Satan is; where Ichabod is the mascot of the local university, meaning the glory of the Lord has departed; and which is the acknowledged world capital of that organized system of witchcraft and idolatry known as modern psychiatry. Topeka comes from the word Topage, or Tophet, which means hell."

More often, they would be delivered to the nation at large: "God has duped Bush into a bloody war in Iraq. They turned America over to fags; they're coming home in body bags. God himself duped Bush into a no-win war by putting a lying spirit in the mouths of all his trusted advisors—to punish America."

Now and then they ranged into genuinely incomprehensible territory, as in one sermon where his refrain of "You're gonna eat your babies!" went viral on YouTube as an example of how deranged Fred Phelps really could be. His rant was about how desperate people were in many corners of the globe, and that the reason was humanity's godless behavior. But "eat your babies" . . . I could never really explain it whenever anyone asked me about that, nor the phrase "Bitch Burger" that went along with it. It sure grabbed people's attention on placards, though.

Another favorite topic with Gramps was predestination—the idea that it had already been decided, when you were born, whether you were bound for heaven or hell. Since you could never know, you were supposed to behave as if you were bound for heaven—and hope for the best. But Gramps had it on good authority, he said, that his congregation was destined for glory, much like Noah and his family. When the Rapture came, he would tell us, the group who would be saved would be very small, only a remnant of society. In one sermon, he specified eight as the number of people who got on Noah's Ark—which struck abject fear into the hearts of his congregation. In our Bible study later that week, my aunt Marge broke down crying. "All I know is, when the Lord comes and if there's only eight people who go," she sobbed, "I want to be one of those eight people." None of us really knew how to comfort her, either. We all hoped to be one of those eight people, too, and there were a lot more than eight of us in the church.

There was a never-ending supply of subject matter for Gramps to preach about, since there were always world events that confirmed his belief that mankind was doomed. And Gramps was sharp; he was a good debater. He knew the Bible cover to cover and he could out-argue anyone. Often his sermons would remind you that he'd been a practicing lawyer—he could sound like he was making an extended closing argument in the case of WBC versus The Rest of Civilization.

Since the service would often take two hours, toward the end we tried not to fidget and looked forward to when Gramps would pick up his tall glass of water to take a drink, indicating the sermon was finished. At the end of the service, Uncle Tim would go back up and everyone would stand and sing another hymn. Then Gramps would say, "And when they had sung a hymn, they went out," per a Biblical verse. We'd file out.

Every so often, we would have a baptism, when someone wanted to officially become a member of the church. Unlike many Christian religions, our baptism wasn't performed when we were a baby; it was when we were old enough to make the decision for ourselves that we wanted to be a member. After all, Gramps said, Jesus was an adult when he was baptized.

My own decision to join the church came, as did many events in my life, with a mixture of laughter and terror. My brother Ben and I shared the trait of reacting to uncomfortable situations with giggles. I had mentioned joining the church to Gramps, and one day when Ben and I were driving in his blue Geo Metro to a picket, he asked me, "Why do you want to be a member of the church?"

"Because I don't want to go to hell!" I blurted out in a rush. He laughed at me, which made me laugh at myself.

BAPTISMS COULD TAKE PLACE INDOORS OR OUTDOORS, depending on the weather; inside the chapel, there was a curtained mahogany baptismal pool up front, near where my dad played the piano. When I was baptized at sixteen, it was summer, so we used the swimming pool.

Gramps had a specific sermon he used just for baptisms, when he reminded us that we were committing our lives to Jesus and the church and to serving God. Following his sermon, he announced, "Libby has expressed that she wants to be a member of the church. She has a good heart."

Everyone went out to the pool, and Gramps took his place at the side, holding a sweatband in his hand. He waded into the water with his black water socks, dark blue shorts, and black T-shirt, and beckoned me to follow in my black and pink athletic shorts and T-shirt. As we stood waist-deep in the turquoise water, he put an arm around my back, putting the sweatband over my face and dipping me back into the water, so I was completely immersed in it. Bringing me back up, he said, "I baptize you my daughter in the name of the Father, the Son, and the Holy Spirit into newness of life."

After every baptism came the Lord's Supper, where everybody would drink from one wine cup and eat unleavened bread, both of which had been blessed by Gramps. "Anyone who eats or drinks unworthily is going to hell," he would remind us. I was always a little afraid I would choke on the bread or the wine and start coughing, but thankfully I never did.

Our everyday behavior outside the church was almost as important as what went on inside every Sunday. We were charged to always be thankful that we had been chosen as the Lord's elect. As such, bad moods were not allowed. Period. If we woke up on the wrong side of the bed, we just had to act like we hadn't, and put a smile on our face. If my mom could sense that I was cranky, she would give me space, telling my siblings and father, "Don't disrupt Libby, she's in a bad mood today." They would all make a really big deal out of it; if we weren't being cheerful, we weren't being helpful to the church. "If you're in a bad mood," they would say, "your heart is in the wrong place." And if we ever acted cranky before going to a picket, watch out. "Shape up!" Shirl would be quick to snap. "You can't go out there looking like that." We always had to be cheery. If you look at any of the videos of our pickets, you'll notice that all of us are always smiling and singing and happy. This was no accident. Even if we weren't delighted to be out there—and how could we be, when we were doing it every day of our lives?—we had to look like we were.

But the good-mood mandate worked. Unfailingly, journalists and media people who came regularly to gawk at us would write with surprise about what nice, nice people we were, how friendly and considerate and polite when we weren't holding signs and yelling slogans. Of course, this was partially true: As Midwesterners, we were brought up to be nice. But we always had an underlying fear of getting a talking-to if we were caught scowling or shirking our duties or in any way suggesting that our lifestyle was anything but joyous, 24/7.

Even though Shirl always spouted that everyone should act the same no matter what—i.e., we hold the world to the Bible's standards (WBC standards) so we have to hold ourselves to it—she in particular acted differently around the media. When British investigative journalist Louis Theroux came to do his documentary on us, she said something like, "We have to be nice to them because they're gonna get all of our words and put it on display for the whole world to see" in a sing-song voice, with a crazy smile on her face and clapping her hands to the rhythm of the words.

If you follow the WBC's pickets, it may strike you that they can always find someone or something to accuse of ungodliness—there's a never-ending list of offenders for them to protest. The inner workings of the church were very similar. The elders will find fault with a person, and when that situation is resolved to their satisfaction, they'll scan the rest of the group in search of another insignificant issue to find fault with and "correct." They rebuke one another—I was told sometimes that to "rebuke" means to show honor. It also means to bring something to light and expose it, and shame the person into doing right. Rebuking our own family members was a regular practice among the WBC, as a means of keeping the group on the path of righteousness.

CHORES WERE ONE WAY WE WERE SUPPOSED TO SERVE THE church—the servants of God—in order to serve God. At least my generation didn't have to go door to door selling candy, like the kids in my dad's generation did. While Gramps was still working as a layman to earn a living—he even sold vacuum cleaners door to door at one point—he decided that the kids should help support the church by selling candy. Gramps would buy it wholesale from a distributor and assign the kids to different areas to knock on doors and sell it. Recently, I met a woman from Topeka who remembered that time. She said she'd been a child then, and her mother had gotten mad at the Phelps children who'd rung their doorbell. She threatened to call the police. I guess they'd just constantly been returning to the houses nearest to them, trying again and again to sell candy. She remembered feeling sorry for them because she could see the fear and disappointment in their eyes.

When I was younger, starting around the age of eight, my chores consisted mostly of babysitting or helping my mom with her day-care business. As I got older, they expanded to gardening on the block, picking up sticks and any trash, making our block look respectable. When I got my driver's license, I would be put in charge of transporting some of the younger kids to pickets. I was a good swimmer, so I was also charged with giving swimming lessons to the other kids. Anyone who was having trouble with reading or math in school could arrange to be tutored by an older kid; we used the nursery room, which the very little kids stayed in if their fussiness couldn't be controlled during church services, as a tutoring center during the week.

Early on, I noticed there was a difference in the distribution of chores. Shirley's kids never seemed to have to do quite as much as everyone else, getting preferential treatment in terms of the cushiest jobs. I never resented Megan too much because she was my best friend, but I knew that Shirley didn't like me and I felt like she enjoyed assigning me harder tasks. I am sure, if you asked her, she would say she always knew I was going to leave the church, and that she had no room in her heart for reprobate sinners like me who were masquerading as true believers. Maybe she would even be right.

IN THE EARLY 2000S, AS I GOT INTO MY LATE TEENS, THE church's rules regarding women began to change and increase in severity, echoing the edicts of Islam and orthodox Judaism in their insistence on women's subservience to men. For many years, there were certain rules we had to follow as women, though none of them seemed especially onerous. We had to wear head coverings in church out of humility before God. And women were never allowed to give sermons or to speak in church. That was just the way it had always been. Besides, it was usually only Gramps—and sometimes my uncle Tim and in later years the other married men of the church—who ever did any talking in church, anyway. We didn't think too much about it.

Around the same time, Gramps had started making changes in the church rules as well. I got the feeling he was pushed into it by Steve Drain, who with his family had joined the church and was always trying to impress the church elders with his devotion to piety. He had been instrumental in kicking his own daughter out for sneaking around and messing with boys, and now he seemed to want to push the church in a more extreme direction. Gramps, who was slowing down a bit in his old age, was happy to let him and some of the other men make some more of the decisions.

Soon afterward, power began to be taken away from Shirl and Marge, who for years had been instrumental in organizing church life and maintaining its public image. It didn't surprise me, nor did the news that Gramps himself was being pushed aside by more radical members. In 2007, WBC members started actively saying that Gramps had lost faith; sweet, humble Gran got on the wrong side of the elders for standing by her husband; she was deemed by Shirl, Steve, and their adherents to be in the wrong for submitting to and supporting her husband. We were told not to talk to Gramps, as we had been forced to do so often in the past when the more outspoken elders deemed other church members' behavior wrong. Gramps wrote a letter to his congregation, which I never read for myself, but I was told it contained words denouncing Shirl, blaming her for what he thought was the church's imminent demise. Shortly afterward, I heard Gramps was excommunicated from the church. He died on March 19, 2014, separated from nearly all of his family.

As for me, people I know today wonder how I could have said and done the things I did, but I was living in an entirely different world with entirely different concepts. I know many people have called it a cult, but even after all these years, and all the changes I've made in myself and my views, I can't bring myself to think that it was. It was just the family I was born into.

CHAPTER TWO

FORMATIVE YEARS

"WATCH YOUR KIDS! GAYS IN RESTROOMS."

That was the sign that started it all. Hand-lettered by Gramps, the sixteen by twenty-inch Styrofoam placard was handed around to all the grownups for inspection. They held it along with other signs at our first picket, which became the event that would forever define Gramps and the church. And it was all in response to a mysterious incident that had taken place one week earlier.

On that day, a warm May afternoon, I had been playing with my cousins on the playground at the family block, as we nearly always did after being dismissed from church. While we raced around the lawn playing tag, the grownups huddled at the stone picnic table, having an intense discussion. We all noticed what was happening, but there was an ironclad rule that we didn't interrupt the adults when they were meeting. We were expected to be respectful and obedient of our elders, and to be as little trouble as possible. One of the advantages of having so many cousins was that we were able to amuse and govern ourselves; there was always at least one kid old enough to supervise the group.

Today, though, I was keeping more of an eye on the adults than I was on the younger children. All of our parents gathered around the table while Gramps and Gran squeezed onto the wooden benches; it was a bigger gathering than usual for a non-Sunday. As usual, though, Gramps looked like he was leading the discussion; Shirl was chiming in and gesticulating energetically.

At eight years old, I could tell a serious discussion when I saw one. The adults' conversation was hushed; they didn't want us to hear exactly what was going on. They rubbed their brows and looked upset, occasionally glancing over at us; we didn't need to hear the words to know something was up.

I looked at my cousins, wide-eyed, afraid to actually say anything about the situation for fear of being reprimanded. By tacit agreement, we all ran across the lawn and resumed playing tag, far enough away that the adults wouldn't be bothered by it.

That night, my parents told us what they had found out from Gramps. He had been biking through nearby Gage Park with six-year-old Josh that day when something bad had happened. A man in the park had done something that had apparently made Gramps mad.

"What did he do?" I asked repeatedly. My parents wouldn't tell me the specifics. They would only say that the man had been a homosexual, and that he had wanted to lure my cousin away, and that the park was filled with like-minded evil men who were engaged in depraved acts and were dangerous around kids. I was shocked, though I didn't really know what "homosexual" meant. I assumed it was simply a scary man who wanted to hurt children. To think that something so awful was happening so near to our house! And how lucky it was that Gramps had been there to protect my little cousin!

It was only later that I found out the whole story. Josh and Gramps had been riding together in the park—Josh, on training wheels, trailing behind Gramps, who would ride ahead on his bicycle and then circle back around Josh. They had biked down a path that bordered a wooded area in the park, Gramps in the lead, when Josh spotted a man walking out of the woods in their direction. When Gramps circled back to Josh, the man turned around and retreated back into the trees.

That was the extent of it.

Mundane as it was, the incident brought the fire out in Gramps, charging him with a newfound energy and purpose. He'd thought before that the area was a congregating area for gay men, but now he'd seen what he believed was proof— with his grandson in tow, no less. It didn't matter that nothing predatory had actually happened. The incident clarified for Gramps that homosexuality was taking root in Topeka, and he meant to do something about it. Meanwhile, much as in the game of telephone, the more the story got told in our family, the more predatory the man in it became. Soon, they were outright lurking in the bushes, waiting to capture my cousin and drag him away.

After that meeting in the backyard, Gramps decided to let the town officials in Topeka know about the situation and ask them what they planned to do. He wrote a letter to the mayor, in his typical no-holds-barred style.

"Dear Friends," it read. "A malodorous sore with the scab off is open and running at the extreme southwest corner of Gage Park. It is a wooded area with footpaths and bush-shrouded coverts affording privacy for indecent conduct. 'At any hour of the day or night,' a park official told me, 'male couples may be seen entering and exiting the area.' My children, grandchildren, and I are offended and embarrassed by this flagrant situation as we bike and jog in the park. . . . My question: Do you think Gage Park's running sore could be permanently fixed?"

Meanwhile, he enlisted all of us to help make small signs to hold up around Gage Park. He and my aunts and uncles figured all the Topeka residents, especially the local church officials, would realize what was going on in the park and join in the fight. The exact opposite happened. The majority of Topekans ridiculed, marginalized, and demonized us; church officials were the most outspoken. Mayor Butch Felker wrote a letter in response to Gramps, agreeing there was a problem, but failing to propose any solutions or take any actions.

Outraged, Gramps started to attend and speak at city council meetings regularly, sometimes bringing us grandchildren with him. I was very excited to be included in these important missions, helping my grandfather fight the injustice of a situation about which he was so obviously right. (Plus, he would give us change to buy candy in the vending machines.) He also wrote letters to the city asking them to cleanse the park of homosexuals. No one heeded them, adding fuel to the fire of his campaign.

It was here that Gramps's righteous cause really began to take shape. People always ask me why Westboro focused so exclusively on gay people. I genuinely think it was mostly because Gramps spied a niche for his church, an evangelical crusade that could only be made better the angrier people got about it. It was also a Biblical sin that had clearly been outlined in the Leviticus story of Sodom and Gomorrah. When someone would point out the many other laughable "sins" in the Bible designated for drastic punishment, like wearing clothing woven from two kinds of cloth, we would always tell them that those things fell under ceremonial law, which the New Testament did away with, while sodomy fell under moral law, which it hadn't. (The fact that we weren't picketing about many other now-accepted "sins" on the list of moral laws—like working on the Sabbath, or rebellion against one's parents—was irrelevant, Gramps would say; he maintained that homosexuality was the one sin that American culture was most aggressively and dangerously trying to promote.)

The pickets started in 1991, once a week at Gage Park. The very first time we picketed, we were a group of about twenty gathered by the park's main 10th Street entrance, on a nice day with a warm, gentle summer breeze. Gramps stood in the middle of our group, clad in his KU windbreaker and running shorts; he hadn't yet started to wear the cowboy hat that would become one of his most recognizable accessories. Only the adults held the GAYS IN RESTROOMS signs, along with GAY PARK and others; we stood alongside them, trying not to fidget. Gramps rationalized that it only made sense to have the kids along at the pickets, given that they were at the center of his campaign to purge the homosexual menace from the park. And, as in church, he believed children were never too young to start learning about what made God angry. You never knew when a child would begin understanding what they were being told, so they needed to be told early and often about wrong and right—and what we should be fighting for.

The Topeka cops, whom Shirl had notified in advance of our presence, instructed us to keep on the move; local law dictated that we could only hold a protest if we didn't stay in one place. So we walked around in a big circle until the grass wilted, before moving on to another circle. At first it was just us, standing by the side of the road, but within half an hour, as people began to pay attention to our signs as they drove by, we got our first reactions. Someone flipped their middle finger up at us and honked angrily. I raised my eyebrows in disbelief and looked over at Josh and Jacob, wide-eyed. How rude! Nobody in our family ever made that gesture, though I'd learned what it meant, as most kids did, from conversations at school. "Fuck you," someone else yelled out of a car window. Gramps stood firm, smiling ferociously out at the world from behind his sign, assured of the rightness of his cause. It was contagious; we began to enjoy the backlash we got, confident that it was coming from people who didn't know the first thing about being godly.

Over the next few weeks, we ramped up our picketing schedule and protested most afternoons at the 10th Street entrance. In addition to the spiteful comments we got from people driving by, someone mooned us out of a truck window one afternoon. "Don't look at that," my mother said hurriedly when it happened, putting her arms around me and Sara and directing us away from the road. But we had seen, and we giggled about it later with Megan. It was the first time either of us had seen a grownup's naked rear end. People in the outside world were so weird, we decided. What normal person would do something that gross? And to a group of God-fearing Christians who were just trying to do the right thing?

Regular counter-protestors appeared with their own signs. Other churches started picketing—against us! They carried signs that answered back to ours, with slogans like GOD LOVES EVERYONE—which, we knew from Gramps's sermons, was definitely not the case. And their signs definitely weren't up to WBC's standards. White background with boring red writing—how was that supposed to grab anyone's attention compared to our multicolored, eye-popping signs?

It wasn't long before there were enough people in the counter-protests that the men in our group made the decision to link arms to create a barrier against the angry masses. Shirl and the others decided to make light of the situation and nickname the various members of the throng who, they had decided, wanted to kill us.

A woman across the street, who seemed always to be wearing violet-hued outfits as she yelled back at us, became "Purple Pig." A large woman who would drive a tiny tan pickup truck past us and give us the finger became "Sun Block." Both names seemed a little hypocritical given how many of my aunts and uncles tended to be on the larger side, but I would never have dared point this out. "Witch," "Karl the Fat Fag," and "Church Whore" were among the other slurs they came up with for the various townspeople who opposed us. This was the beginning of a long tradition of mocking those who came out against us publicly.

The rhythm of a picket quickly became second nature. We would show up with our signs and people would drive and walk by, yelling or cursing at us, or worse. The adults—especially Gramps—would just smile and laugh in response, safe in the knowledge that God was on their side and would provide divine protection. So we learned to react that way too. Soon enough, I was hardened to all manner of R-rated insults, and had learned to smile them down.

During those first weeks, Gramps preached in church that what we were doing on the streets of Topeka was a loving gesture. That the way to love your neighbor was to rebuke them; to help them see the error of their ways and turn to God. It was only later that I figured out that Gramps didn't really expect anyone outside of the church to change their ways—that it was us, and us alone, who were the chosen servants of God.

UNTIL THE YEAR WE BEGAN PICKETING, MY LIFE DIDN'T SEEM all that different from any other Kansas kid. I was born in 1983, the year Cabbage Patch Dolls came out, and the running joke among my relatives was how much I looked like one, with my chubby face and dimples. I grew up in a comfortable house, on the large side of average, on a leafy street named Holly Lane, within easy walking distance of all the other family members and church. Life revolved around school, church, and playing with my siblings and cousins on the "block." My grade school was a five-minute walk from the house, so every morning, Megan, Josh, and Jacob would come by for me and Sara, and all of us would go together. In many ways, we were pretty regular kids. We loved playing sports, especially volleyball, which helped us fit in and was a distraction from the ways in which we were different. I had friends from school over to the house in those days, though I didn't get to have those playdates as frequently as most kids did. I also had never cut my hair, which made me, my sister, and my female cousins a bit of a curiosity. The other kids frequently asked why we never cut our hair. "Because the Bible says not to!" we would respond, shocked they didn't know this already.

Hair was one of the ways that people in Topeka knew we were Phelps girls, by our long, long braids or ponytail, or big bun. By the time I was ten, my hair was all the way past my butt. So was Sara's and Jael's, and all the other cousins too, except for Megan, whose hair was entirely too curly and barely passed her shoulders. We were proud of our long hair, and took good care of it. I washed mine every single day and brushed it meticulously, and then I would always put it up in a bun. It was easier than having to deal with a fancy haircut, and we didn't have to use hair products. Sometimes Megan would

French braid my hair; I enjoyed the style and the time we were able to sit and talk.

The church always played a bigger role in our lives than it did in those of most of the kids I knew. Nearly everyone at school went to a church of some kind, but nobody else had their own grandfather for a minister or had their very own family chapel. And the dramatic, graphic lessons we learned on Sundays—TULIP, the aspects of hell, predestination—were a lot more stringent than the typical Christian sermons being preached in Topeka's typical Midwestern Methodist churches.

In 1995, a few years after the picketing had started, I began to notice a difference in how I was treated at middle school. Kids didn't like me anymore. They didn't talk to me like they used to, and they openly whispered about me while I was near them. I no longer had an assured place with my friends in the cafeteria. I sat with my sister and cousins when we had the same lunch period.

I had been prepared for this for years; Gramps had been preaching about it since I was three. God's elect would be persecuted, and there was no better place for persecution than middle school.

We grew up in the shadow of our parents, aunts, and uncles having been mocked mercilessly at school for being related to a crusading civil rights lawyer. Gramps's being the one attorney in Topeka who regularly represented black clients didn't make him overly popular in the informally segregated town in the 1960s, and my uncle Tim used to tell us about how he was beaten up by kids at school for having, as he reported they'd said, a "nigger-lover" for a father. So Gramps always raised his kids to accept, and even cherish, being seen as different from the other kids—and that mindset was passed down to us as we were increasingly trained to see the entirety of the outside world as sinful.

I had been warned this was coming, and I tried not to let it get to me—I wanted to wear their judgment like a badge of honor, just as Gramps had instructed. I really did feel special for having been chosen by God to suffer affliction for His sake. There was something so rewarding knowing we were 100 percent right and everyone else was wrong. I wasn't afraid of the world—I was sorry for everyone else, because they had no idea what was in store for them. Even if we told them a million times they were going to hell, they didn't believe it. My sister Sara didn't share my feelings; being ostracized at school got to her early, and she was quietly miserable.

But when we were at home, life was an oasis—especially compared to Gramps's weekly fire-and-brimstone sermons and the rocky terrain of middle school. My father may have been Fred Phelps's eldest son, but he hadn't inherited much of Gramps's temperament. My parents were both quiet people, not given to yelling or big displays of emotion. They would usually show their displeasure with us by just giving us the silent treatment—and they showed their affection for us sparingly. (I would only learn later in life that this was not what it was like for everyone growing up.) They didn't hug us very much, and kisses were all but unheard of, at least as soon as we were old enough to be out of diapers. A backrub was about as much intimacy as we could hope for from either of them. Sometimes my parents felt like vaguely detached caretakers: We knew they had our best interests at heart, but we also knew we had to follow the rules in order to stay in their good graces. Politeness—and godliness, of course—was key. From a very young age, I was always on guard against upsetting, annoying, or disappointing them. Being ignored—or worse, shamed—by them felt worse to me than getting screamed at (which was what you could expect if you were one of Shirl's eleven kids).

My mother, following the teachings of conservative Christianity, was submissive to my father as the head of the household. Anything my dad, or the church, told her, she would do without question. She was also infinitely patient, which would serve her well when she started running a day care at our house several years after I was born. My father wasn't as patient with us. He was quiet, but we could tell by his tensed face, fidgeting fingers, and quicker breathing he was getting irritated with us. He also wasn't around nearly as much as my mom. When I was little, he worked as a parole officer, so he wasn't home much; later, he became a staff attorney with the Kansas Department of Corrections, a position he holds to this day.

When he was home, he didn't speak to us all that much. He was a germaphobe, washing his hands constantly, and he didn't want to have anything to do with changing diapers—one of his favorite phrases was "Get that away from me!" Certainly, he wanted nothing to do with his kids if we were ever coughing or sneezing or had stomachaches, as was bound to happen in a house with four children. But he did love sports and liked to throw a baseball or shoot baskets with us.

He was often away on business and had to stay in a hotel in Wichita, or other places too far away to make the daily drive. Years later I learned he had had his lawyer's license suspended, for his involvement in the case that got Gramps' federal law license revoked entirely, and subsequently had trouble finding work near home. He would take an air mattress with him because the motel beds were too uncomfortable (and, given his germaphobia, possibly because of the fear of touching a motel bed) and return late the following evening, so we would regularly go several days without seeing him.

My mom didn't fear germs like my dad did, but health was a big obsession with both of them. While junk food and premade dishes were popular in our extended family—Gramps loved having Subway sandwiches on hand in his fridge, while Shirl was always heating up premade eggrolls and baking cookies from packaged dough—my mom was a good cook who made most things from scratch. Our house always smelled of freshly baked bread or something else scrumptious cooking in the oven. Making bread, kneading it, and rolling it out on our wooden dining room table was one of my and Sara's favorite activities. My mom was good at including us in everything, making us feel we were a part of things. She may not have hugged us very often, but she made us feel loved and wanted.

MY PARENTS SCRUPULOUSLY FOLLOWED THE PRECEPTS OF THE church—including, increasingly, not allowing us to socialize with any kids outside of the church unless it was for a school project—but they were still a constant target for scrutiny within the church. My dad had married an outsider, which made them both suspect. Everyone is always watching someone in the church, and Shirl especially made it her business to keep tabs on the way my mom was raising us. If she saw something she didn't think was right, she didn't hesitate in upbraiding her for it. "Dr. Spock is your god," she would sneer at my mother if she tried some modern parenting technique. If we were acting up, my even-tempered mom was more inclined to rationalize with us instead of immediately concluding our hearts were in the wrong place and that we were children of the devil—as Shirl did with her children. If my mom read up on natural remedies for us, Shirl would tell her, "You need to trust in the Lord." There was a standard my mother was supposed to be following, and it wasn't written down any-where—she had to figure it out through trial and error, being scolded for her errors by Shirl. When I got a little older, I began to get picked on for being part of the church, so I went home and talked to my mom about it. "It's not like we always talk about religion," I told her. "Yes," she agreed, "it's a big part of our lives, but it's not everything." She didn't shove religion down our throats every day like Shirl did; she acted kind and respectful toward everyone.

My brother Ben, much older than me, used to get in trouble with the aunts and uncles too for being too silly. "How is that serving God?" they'd scold him. But it never got him down. Even if a lot of his humor was at my expense, I was glad to have someone in the family who liked to laugh. He did get me in trouble a lot when he'd sneakily say something very quietly to me, to which I would respond loudly. My parents did not like loudness.

DESPITE THEIR BEST EFFORTS, I TENDED TO BE BETTER FRIENDS with my rowdy boy cousins than the quieter girls. My sister and I would play with Barbie dolls and our Snoopy snow cone maker, but I preferred to be out running around with the boys than playing what I thought of as girly games. Plus, the boy cousins were closer to my age, and when I tried to hang around with Sara and our church friend Katherine, they just looked at me as the little sister who kept pestering them.

All the kids, whatever their ages, had a reliable source of kindness in our grandmother, who was more affectionate than my parents and whose doors were always open to us. Sweet, tiny Gran was always very gentle and motherly. She never shamed me when I didn't know something, and always helped me with anything I needed, from homework to Bible questions to, later on, advice about becoming a woman.

She was a counterpoint to Gramps, an example of kindness and gentleness at its finest. I always felt so secure and safe around her (even during the church's "intervention" directed at me, much later on, when I felt the whole world was against me). Sometimes, when Gramps would go on an hour or more with his religious ramblings, she would take pity on me. In her mild but effective way, she'd prevail on him to stop so I could leave.

Our favorite weekend activity was sleepovers at Gran and Gramps's place. Megan, Josh, Jacob, and I would line up our sleeping bags together in the brown-carpeted fireplace room, and binge on all kinds of delicious junk food. Our favorite dish was nachos with Old El Paso sauce and shredded cheese, for which we'd rinse the chips off with water to remove the salt and to make them softer for Gran. Her teeth didn't work very well, and we didn't mind if the chips were a little bendy. For dessert, there'd be ice cream and Milky Ways. Sitting at the kitchen table behind heaping bowls of ice cream, we'd watch Gran play solitaire, eventually catching on and learning how to play ourselves. Sometimes she would show us old jewelry, and once she even gave me one of her old rings that, many years later, I would wear when I got married. Those sleepovers were one of the rare occasions when we didn't really talk about religion. I look back on them as being one of the only times we got to just be kids and have fun.

There weren't many moments like that. We got to go to the park or skating rink, play sports, go to the movies and out to dinner, and go clothes and music shopping, but we almost always had the responsibility of watching over the younger kids. Fun activities turned out to be not quite as fun when we

GIRL ON A WIRE

had to constantly monitor the little ones; I was always worried they would run off somewhere or start screaming and make a scene, and then I would get reprimanded for it. We were also burdened with being in the public eye. People recognized us when we went out—if they didn't know us personally, they could tell by the girls' long hair. (There were occasional advantages to having my hair as long as it was, though. Later on, in middle school, everyone was busy coloring their hair. We weren't allowed to do any such thing, of course, but because my hair reached nearly all the way down my back, I could grab a lock of it and color it with pink highlighter. I liked that look.)

JUST AS WE WEREN'T ALLOWED TO CUT OUR HAIR, WE CERTAINLY weren't allowed any kind of cosmetics. The assumption by our elders was that we must be trying to attract attention by wearing makeup, rather than just doing it because it was fun, because everybody else was doing it, because school was boring. Every move any of us made that stepped outside the bounds of the church was seen as having an ulterior motive—and someone (usually Shirl) was going to get to the bottom of it.

But one day my sister Sara rebelled. She bought a bottle of red nail polish at the Walgreens in Topeka and painted her nails one night when nobody was looking. The next morning, she came down to breakfast wearing gloves. "Why do you have gloves on while you're eating toast?" my mom asked. Sara claimed she was cold. Later, when she came home from school and my mom saw the polish, she just laughed—which was very unlike what would have happened had she been one of Shirl's kids.

With Shirl, we knew you had to walk on eggshells or risk a tongue-lashing, or worse. With Gramps, it depended on the day. Much of the time, he was a doting grandfather to us—unless you did something he considered stupid or ignorant, and then he'd let us have it, in that thunderous voice of his. We all lived in fear of having Gramps call us dumb, a mark of shame. But I loved it when he would jokingly call me a "Troublemaker" or say, "Here comes trouble" when I entered a room. He said it so much that when I was clothes shopping and saw a black shirt with TROUBLEMAKER written in glittery white cursive writing, I couldn't resist buying it.

Often, though, he would play with us like any other grandpa. He seemed like a different person when he was outside of the church. In the afternoons, when we got home from school, he would come out to the block, dressed in his track suit, and join in whatever we were doing. In the summer, he'd jump into the huge swimming pool and play Marco Polo with us. But his favorite activity was running, a holdover from his younger years. Gramps had been a great hurdler and had always been convinced that his family needed to be in good shape to be "fit for the battle." When I was five, *Runner's World* magazine even did a story about Gramps's obsession with running and his strict regimen for his kids, which included making them run several miles every day and even more on the weekends when they had more time. He had mellowed by the time my generation came around, but he still encouraged all us kids to get into the habit of running as much as possible. Down the street from our house, there was a little circular park; when I was at a loss for something to do, my dad would say to me, "Run down to the circle and run around it ten times." I don't remember ever objecting to this, or thinking it was too harsh. I liked to play sports and I liked to be outside. But there was a larger reason for Gramps's emphasis on physical fitness: The running was so we would be in shape to fight the holy war.

He didn't make us do daily runs, like he'd once done with his own kids, but he did encourage us to run races around the track in the backyard. One afternoon, I won a race against my cousins, and to celebrate, Gramps picked me up and put me on the stone picnic table. I burst into tears, because I didn't want to be the center of attention. Gramps thought that was really funny and reminded me of this story often as I grew up.

This sort of devotion to the church, in body and in mind, dictated many of the unofficial rules that governed our family. Pets, for example, were frowned upon as a waste of valuable time, which could be better spent serving the Lord. Despite that edict, though, my family got away with having many of them over the years: a cat named Flufferbuns (an odd name chosen by my dad), a rabbit named Bugs, a hamster named Toby. We even had chickens at one point.

My dad's favorites were our dogs, though: Sunshine, Cosmo, and Newman—the latter two after *Seinfeld*, which my whole family loved, especially Ben. My sister also had a little Westie named April. The big dogs were outside dogs, so they lived in their doghouses in the backyard, and my dad loved them more than anybody. (The day Newman got hit by a car was one of the few times I've ever seen him cry. It broke my heart to see him cry. It was a time where a hug was definitely indicated, but historically that was not something we did. I just sat on our brown couch and held back my own tears. I was twenty years old at the time. A few months later, Sunshine got sick. He took her to the vet, but it didn't do any good; she crawled away into the woods one day and died. On a hike one day, my dad and my little nephew Seth found her bones. "I could see all of her ribs," said Seth, always a very unflappable kid.)

Seth was one of the many children my mom would take into her day care at our house, for which she'd given up her job outside the house. Before, she had worked as a lawyer at the family practice, Phelps-Chartered, downtown on Topeka Boulevard. All of the church members of her generation had been encouraged to get law degrees, and if you were a direct relative of Fred Phelps, it was almost an order. Later on, he'd say, "God knew this picketing ministry would happen—so he prepared us by sending us all to law school."

Back in the years when I was too young to go to school, my mother took me into the office with her during the day. If clients came in, I'd simply play under the desk, poking my head out to stare at the strangers and then scurrying back underneath if they noticed me.

One of my earliest memories is from those days, an occasion when Shirl came storming into my mother's office. She was mad about a difference of opinion she and my mom had on a case Phelps-Chartered was representing, and her anger quickly got personal, as it usually did. From early on she'd made it clear she didn't like my mom, and she took every opportunity to take her to task about the littlest things. My mother, even-tempered in a way that tended to make Shirl even more furious, scooped me up immediately and headed for our blue Toyota van in the parking lot; she didn't want me around Shirl when she was throwing one of her fits. Shirl following behind, undeterred and vengeful. "You don't raise your children properly!" she screeched. "You're not doing your duty as a parent!" Outwardly unfazed—though I imagine it must have gotten to her—my mom calmly drove us home. She was good at not letting Shirl into our home life, a tall order considering how closely we all lived. Later on, I knew that a blowup like this meant I likely wouldn't be allowed to talk to Megan for a while—that was how Shirl operated. She knew taking away my best friend was the worst punishment for me, so that was what she did.

From as far back as I can recall, I always instinctively disliked Shirl. Everything was either her way or the highway. I was afraid to speak or even move around her; I yearned to get by her unnoticed. Some family members liked to say I had a temper like Gramps, or like my aunt Abi, but no one ever said I was like Shirl—and I was always glad of that. Her anger would cause my autonomic nervous system to kick in, fight-or-flight at its finest, increased respirations, increased heart rate. She made us feel like there was nothing we could do right; nothing would ever please her. So I kept my distance as much as I could, and tried to be obedient and helpful when I couldn't.

WHEN I STARTED SCHOOL FULL-TIME, MY MOM STOPPED working and watched kids, ones from both inside and outside of the church. I was expected to help her when I got home from school, but I was also allowed to go to the block to play.

Running, freeze tag, volleyball, basketball, playing on what we referred to as the "big toy"—a jungle gym—and tetherball were all regular activities in the afternoons. When it was warm enough, we could usually be found swimming in the pool and making up competitions to see who could do the silliest dive. Still, the church would always seep into the fun. If we wanted to mess with someone, we'd say, "You are a liar of the devil, and the truth is not in you," or maybe call them a heathen. If there had been a sermon that week on a particularly scary aspect of the afterlife—as there often was—it was on the block that we'd hash its meaning out between us. Because the adults put so much emphasis on getting doctrine right, and not appearing stupid, arguments would inevitably break out about who was the most correct and who had learned their Bible lessons the best. When fights did happen, it was an unspoken rule that Shirl's kids were never wrong, so even if we weren't the one who hit the other kid, it was best to just take the blame.

I took a lot of blame over the years. Maybe it was partly because of Shirl's feelings about my mother, but even at a young age I remember feeling like I could never do enough to make my elders happy. It didn't help that I often looked upset. It was my own misfortune to have been born with what I have since learned is called "resting bitch face." Even as a toddler, I would sit in church services concentrating very hard, and I would be told I looked like I was glaring at everyone. To this day, when I'm not actively smiling, people think I'm scowling. This did not make me popular with the aunts and uncles, especially Shirl, who had made it one of her missions to enforce the church edict about everybody being in a good mood—or at least looking like it—all the time.

ONE PLACE I DID RELIABLY HAVE FUN WAS AT OUR FAMILY parties. We never celebrated religious holidays, because Gramps said they were all dirty pagan celebrations at their core. He'd quote the book of Jeremiah, warning against "adorning trees with gold and silver," which ruled out Christmas; Easter, with its relationship to pre-Christian fertility rituals, was definitely not for us. For a while, we celebrated the Fourth of July—but that eventually had to go too, once Gramps had decided the military was fighting for a "fag nation."

But we always had a monthly birthday party for whoever was celebrating one that month (with a family the size of ours, there were always at least a couple of birthdays every month). Before the picketing years, we also threw an annual Phelps Family Barbecue. We would rent a bounce house and a portable popcorn machine, and we'd invite all the neighbors and local politicians.

In my early childhood, my father was very involved in local politics—which is always surprising to people who know the church for its stances today. But this was in the years before religion and politics were as linked as they are today, and both my dad and Gramps were proud Democrats for years. One of my favorite family activities was going to "bean feeds," what we called political fundraisers, where we'd have chili and cinnamon rolls, a Kansan specialty. My dad was a real politics nerd, and that was one of the rare subjects I could get him to talk to me about, other than sports.

One of my earliest memories is of a big fundraiser we threw at our house in 1988 for Al Gore, who was running for president. He and Joan Finney, who was later the governor of Kansas, came to our party, and I met Mr. Gore. I'm sure he wouldn't be thrilled to be associated with my family now, but at the time he just seemed like a very nice man who enjoyed our Midwestern hospitality.

THE BLOCK, BESIDES BEING OUR PERSONAL PLAYGROUND AND party central, was also where we tried to work out the meaning of some of Gramps's sermons' explanations of homosexuality, which often included terms that we, at such a young age, had never heard of. We would have very inappropriate conversations for grade school–aged kids, nonchalantly throwing around terms such as "butt buddy," "bestiality," and "pedophile perverts," all of which we regularly heard in Gramps' sermons. We didn't exactly understand the extent of what we were saying, but the important thing—as Gramps would say—was that we knew it was all disgusting behavior we didn't want any part of.

"What's a golden shower?" I asked my cousin one day, in between bounces on the trampoline. We would often come out to play after the church service on Sunday, where Gramps so often preached about the dangers of homosexuals and the ungodly things they did. But, as often when I was young, I didn't know the terms he used. I tried never to ask the adults for fear of being laughed at, or told I should have paid better attention or read my Bible more thoroughly. All of these were likely outcomes of being too inquisitive around the grownups, so I tried to pry all the information I could out of Shirl's kids. They tended to know more about these things than I did; Shirl talked a lot more than my parents.

Mariah Carey blasted from Megan's boom box while she and I tried to time our jumps perfectly to make the other jump as high as we could without being flung off onto the lawn. "It's disgusting," she said, "but what I think it is, is when someone pees on another person."

"Gross!" I yelled, coming to a halt on the elastic surface. "That's disgusting! Why would someone do that?"

"I know!" she said, shaking her head. "My mom told me they do it for sexual pleasure."

"Nasty!" I cried, giddy with the sheer outrageousness of it. "That would make me want to throw up!"

The term would be pushed to the back of my mind as we began playing with the littler kids, who would throw Nerf balls at us as we tried to jump and avoid them.

But it would come up again in church the next Sunday, and the next.

NEARLY ALL MY CAREFREE MEMORIES FROM CHILDHOOD ARE intertwined with the terrifying lessons we learned in church from Gramps. On the outside, we were allowed to be kids like anyone else; we ran and played and swam in the pool and chased each other around the trees in endless games of tag. But the conversations we had as kindergarteners, as third graders, as fifth graders, were anything but childlike. We were raised to be constantly afraid of the wrath of God, of Gramps, of Shirl, and of course of the ever-looming threat of going to hell. Not to mention homosexuals, who were out there everywhere just waiting to entice us into their clutches and do depraved things to us, like they did to each other.

Gramps did a lot to keep tabs on the area's homosexual activity, including subscribing to the *Damron Guide*, a publication listing the best meetup and vacation spots for gay people. I felt dirty looking up addresses for Gramps (places to picket when we would go on out-of-town pickets), as my eyes would undoubtedly come across an ad where two men were holding hands, or even worse, kissing! But soon, thanks to all the intrepid scouting, our picketing in Gage Park began to expand to other spots around town that Gramps said had affiliations with gays or gay causes.

Gramps made all the signs in the early picketing years. As we started picketing different locations, he updated his slogans. GAY was soon replaced with FAG because, as Gramps always said, "They're not happy, they're fags; they're bundles of sticks who will fuel the fires of hell." FAG CHURCH was made for all the churches who spoke out against the anti-gay crusade. FAG TPD was made for the Topeka police department because Gramps thought they were part of the gay agenda and didn't protect us adequately when the "fags and fag enablers" harassed us on the picket line.

Once, when I was in my final year of grade school, I was visiting Gramps while he was constructing signs on his dark wooden table that sat in front of the pulpit. The table bore an inscription reading THIS DO IN REMEMBRANCE OF ME in gold letters. I liked to hide under it during games of hide and seek during sleepovers. Gramps laid out a blue Mexican blanket so he didn't scratch the table's surface, leaned over, and drew a perfectly straight line on the "D" in his most famous sign: GOD HATES FAGS. I was impressed with how he could, without a ruler, draw a perfectly straight line. I wanted to help. I wanted to learn how to draw a straight line. I asked if I could work on a sign. He smiled and gave me TURN OR BURN to work on. I got to work on the black outline of the "T," my hand shaking as I was nearing halfway down. I had gone off course. I was terrified. I knew how much these signs meant to Gramps. How was I going to tell him I had messed up one of his signs? I began to panic and started thinking of ways I could fix it before he saw what I had done. I came to the conclusion that I would just make that part of the line thicker. Way thicker than any other letter. I finished the sign and gave it to him, scared of his reaction to the disproportionate thickness of the line I had drawn. He smiled and told me I'd done a good job. There's no way he overlooked my mistake, but I was relieved he didn't point it out. I still wish I could draw a straight line like him.

Despite worrying that I'd make him mad, I loved spending time with Gramps. He was smart and he challenged me, which I have always credited with why I did so well in school. Gramps was also funny; he liked to laugh. He always said what was on his mind, and I have often been told I inherited that trait from him.

When the picketing first started, I especially liked to stand next to Gramps. He had a lot of energy for a grandpa. I would teach him dances, like the Running Man, and we would use the sticks from our signs, which stood on the ground, to balance on while we showed off our moves. Or he would lead a sing-along with one of his early song parodies, like the one he based on "Back in the Saddle Again":

Get back in the closet again
Back where a sin is a sin
Where the filthy faggots dwell
While they're on their way to hell
Get back in the closet again
Preaching the truth once more
Showing the faggots the door
Where the filthy faggots dwell
While they're on their way to hell
Get back in the closet again.

These songs were incredibly catchy, easy for everyone to learn and sing. They also sometimes hit our targets even harder than the mottos on the signs we were carrying. People couldn't believe the lyrics that were coming out of our mouths—especially from the kids.

Making someone at a protest burst into tears didn't happen very often, but when it did, my uncles would laugh. "Yeah, we got somebody to cry!" Brent, Shirl's husband, and Tim would chortle. That made me feel conflicted. I didn't think it was right to make someone cry. I didn't like crying, and I didn't want to make anyone else cry. But seeing my uncles' reaction, I had to quickly change my reaction back to a smile. If we felt differently than the church leaders, we had to keep it to ourselves, or face ridicule for not knowing how to conduct ourselves as a member of God's elect.

MOST OF ALL, WHAT WE DIDN'T WANT TO DO WAS GET GRAMPS mad. Through his sermons, we all knew how fearsome he could be when raging about the godlessness of America. There were rumors—though I'd never seen anything to support them, myself—that he'd hit his kids in earlier days. With the grandkids, though, he was generally patient and kind, unless we did something to raise his ire. I recall once during a church service Gramps got mad at the children for not paying attention. Brent, sitting two pews in front of me, turned around, sat up tall, and slapped one of his sons, Zach, across the face. "He's talking about you!" he angrily and loudly whispered while pointing his finger at him after the slap. Zach was very young, close to ten, but even at that young age, he knew he wasn't supposed to make a sound as he sat there, his face beginning to turn red from the strike.

Once, at a local picket, we were packing up the signs in the back of the white truck that was used for local pickets. I was struggling with a sign that was so big I had to stand on my tiptoes and reach across the back of the truck to lay it in. I stand at a gangly five feet, eight inches, but even so, I had difficulty laying the sign down, and I let it drop the last few inches into the truck. Gramps heard the boards from my sign crash into the sign below.

"What's your problem, girl?" he said in his cutting preacher's voice, as he furrowed his brow over powerful blue-gray eyes. "You've got those long arms, you shouldn't be banging those signs together!" I looked at him, wide-eyed, scared stiff. I was never afraid he would strike me, but verbal lashings from Gramps were worse than any physical punishment I could imagine. His reprimands came quick as lightning and were razor-sharp. But looking in my eyes, he could see that I was terrified and his expression immediately changed—his stern face loosened into a gentle smile. By rule, he never apologized, but I could tell he always felt a little regretful after scolding me.

ONE OF THE VERSES WE'D HEAR A LOT IN THE CHURCH WAS "He that spareth his rod hateth his son; but he that loveth him chasteneth him betimes." Proverbs 13:24. As far as church parents went, mine were pretty lenient in that respect. Gramps would sermonize about how children were supposed to have fear of their parents, but mine didn't spank us very much, maybe partly because we tried really hard to be good, and partly because they just didn't touch us very much in general. I think my mother spanked me with a hairbrush once because I was talking back, but it didn't really hurt that much. Mostly, it would be my dad getting mad and yelling. He was a little scary when he raised his voice. When my mom got mad, she would just stop talking to us.

But there were a couple of incidents that made me wonder if my dad had taken the "spareth his rod" verse to heart. The first was when I was nine years old, in the third grade. My oldest sister, Sharon, had lied to my dad about something petty, and blamed me for it, like most siblings do now and then. I hated when I would get in trouble for something I didn't do, and would defend myself until my last breath. "That's not true, and you know it!" I yelled at her in the kitchen, as I was standing there waiting for something to heat up in the microwave. My father heard and came back into the kitchen with a dark look on his face, and I knew I'd been too loud and sounded too wild. He punched my upper left arm hard—really hard. Tears sprang to my eyes and I tried not to cry, but I was shocked. I had never been hit like that before. The next day at school, I had a huge bruise where he'd punched me. My teacher called me over during a break in class and asked me what happened. I knew my dad would get in trouble if I told her the truth, so I said I didn't remember—I was an active kid, so it was pretty believable that I'd run into something or fallen down while playing.

The next time it happened, I was twelve years old. We had gotten McDonald's for dinner, and I had just helped myself to some French fries when Ben started teasing me, as he did constantly. "You're too fat to have fries, Libby," he said. He would always tell me I was stupid and fat; my mom used to tell me I was fat, too. "Libby Big Butt," they'd call me, or sometimes, less meanly, "Libby Long Legs." I never understood it, because I really wasn't fat, and I knew I wasn't. But it always hurt my feelings anyway.

I threw the handful of fries down on the table in anger, and they spilled onto my dad's placemat. His face hardened instantly. "You'd better get out of here. Right now," my father said in a low voice. I could tell he was furious. I put my food down immediately and ran for the stairs. Terrified, I tried to think of where he wouldn't find me. I went into my brother's bedroom and hid in his closet. Breathing heavily, my heart beating a mile a minute, I heard my father coming upstairs, yelling my name ominously.

It didn't take him long to find me. Opening the closet door, he slapped my face. Hard. Then he grabbed my arm, pulled me out of the closet, and shoved me down the hallway. Trying to run, I reached the stairs and he caught up with me and shoved me again. I tumbled down the carpeted steps, crumpling into a sobbing heap at the bottom. No one else had moved from the table; they were sitting there motionless. My mom had likely told my brother and sister to be quiet and that my dad was in charge. I never threw food onto his placemat again, that was for sure.

ONE OF THE MOST TRAUMATIC INCIDENTS EVER TO HAPPEN AT the block happened when I was thirteen, the summer of 1996. I was playing in the swimming pool with Josh, Jacob, and little Grace, who was only two at the time. Josh, in charge of watching his little sister, shirked his duty by ordering her to go inside and take a nap while we all played games in the deep end of the pool, competing to see who could make the biggest splash off the diving board. As Grace toddled away, we turned back to the game, shrieking and laughing as we jumped into the pool, narrowly missing landing on one another's heads. When we tired of that, Jacob climbed out and ran inside to get popsicles for all of us. I swam toward the shallow end, as it would be challenging to tread water and hold the frozen treat at the same time. As I got to the other end of the pool, I froze: a small body lay on the floor of the pool, just under the water's surface. Scooping Grace into my arms, I reached up and laid her on the ground, cupping her head in my hands so it wouldn't hit the ground too hard. There was a weird purple color underneath her closed eyes and lips; I could see veins all over her face. She didn't seem to be breathing. "Help!" I screamed, leaping out of the water and running into the open kitchen door at Gran and Gramps's house. There was no answer to my shouts. I tore across the yard to Shirl and Brent's house, where there was also no answer. Where was everyone?

I remembered that Tim's wife Lee Ann had just had a baby. Racing to their house, a couple of houses down, I found Tim in the backyard playing with a pack of the cousins with the garden hose, giving his wife a break from their other children to be alone with the new baby. I told him what had happened, and he told me to calm down and sent me into the house to tell Shirl, who was holding the baby, to call 911. When Tim and I got back to the pool, an ambulance was on its way. "Did you hit her head?" he asked. "What?" I asked, surprised. "Did you hit her head!" he asked again, accusingly. "No!" I said, offended by his question. Tim knew I had helped take care of kids for years already; I certainly knew to put my hand on the back of a little kid's head when lying them down. Afterward at the hospital, Brent took me aside to thank me for what I'd done, though Shirl never did say anything to me about it. But what puzzled me, even more than the fact that she never mentioned it, was the fact that God never came up when people talked about the accident. If God was doing so much to punish sinners across the nation—visiting tragedies on people left and right—then why wasn't it the same with us? Why was Grace's near-death an accident instead of a punishment? Once again, I kept my questions to myself. But something felt odd about it, and that feeling didn't go away.

IN 1998, OUR PICKETING WAS GETTING MORE INTENSE AND beginning to turn into a genuine nationwide crusade; the demands of the church seemed to get larger every time you turned around. Gramps and his children started requiring that all families read the Bible at home every night, and gather for regular Bible study groups outside of Sunday services. The kids my age would have to do PowerPoint presentations on the Bible. Mine was on Noah and the flood—a favorite subject of Gramps, who viewed his family, and God's looming destruction of the world, in a similar light. One point in my report that stood out for me was the phrase "And it repented the Lord that he had made man." Did God feel that way about us now? Was he going to end it all again?

I constantly worried I wasn't good enough to be one of God's elect, mostly because of the way Shirl treated me—like I was never good enough. It was terrifying to think the Lord would come and take his elect to heaven and the rest of us would be heading for hell, with the elect administering our punishment.

One thing that we could count on was that our parents, or any adult, would go to the Bible to answer any pressing questions that we kids might have about life or death. Most of what we learned, we learned by absorption instead of by asking outright. This system was how I learned that there was to be no dating or marriage for my generation. I was never specifically told this, but I gathered it from people who were older than me that when all the kids were really young, they collectively decided none of us were going to date.

I also knew almost nothing about getting my period. I knew there would be blood, but I didn't really understand why or how. I asked my mom about it, and my brother Ben was nearby. So he took me aside and told me, "When you get to a certain age, you have to go into the bathroom and stick a needle inside yourself to make yourself bleed." I didn't know any better, and this terrified me until I started my period in the eighth grade. I was scared to use a tampon, because my mother didn't want to discuss them with me, so I just used pads for years until I was seventeen and had to go on a trip to the Bahamas where I'd be wearing a bathing suit.

I knew I couldn't rely on my mom for help, so I went to Gran. At a picket one day, I asked her, "Isn't there something I can do? Take a pill to make it stop?" She just sweetly laughed at me, saying, "You can't mess with that!"

Education about puberty, our bodies, or sex was frowned on in the church. We were never taught about any of it by our parents, though we learned a little bit in the Kansas public school system. At home, we absolutely never talked about sex. I knew that "be fruitful and multiply" means to have a lot of kids, but I learned that from sex education in the fifth grade. When my teacher taught us what sex was, I thought, "That is disgusting. I'm not supposed to be doing that." I knew marriage was supposed to be one man, one woman, one lifetime, but the thought of anyone having sex—eww, gross!

ONE DAY, IN EIGHTH GRADE ENGLISH CLASS, I FELT A TAP ON my shoulder. It was Brandon, a boy who sat behind me. His hands were shaking as he handed me a piece of lined paper. My hand touched his sweaty palm during the transfer. I felt my face turn crimson and immediately wondered why he was so nervous. Was I getting some sort of love note from a boy? This was completely forbidden. I felt my whole body heating up with shame. I opened the paper, and there was my homework from last night. He'd taken it when I wasn't looking and returned it, which, if you're going to be a cheater, was actually a decent thing to do. Thank God, I thought. That was all it was.

That same year brought one of the most humiliating incidents in my entire school career. As I sat in math class, a boy put gum in my hair. I didn't know right away, but when I heard kids giggling behind me I wondered what was up. "Check your hair," one whispered. I put my hand to my head and felt a big gummy mess in my long brown hair. I whipped around. "Why did you do that? This is going to be hard to get out!" I could tell he felt bad for doing it already, but he acted tough.

He said he wanted me to get my hair cut because it was against my religion. It was almost the end of class, and I went to the bathroom, fighting back tears. There was no way to get it out; I rode home on the bus with Sara and she helped me get it out with olive oil. Some of my hair had to be pulled out while we removed the gum. I was terrified of getting in trouble for it, even though it wasn't my fault and we actually didn't cut the hair; I lived with a constant fear of disappointing my parents or, worse, making my dad mad. Even when I broke a dish accidentally I would go into a panic, thinking I'd be in terrible trouble. But when my mom saw the chunk we'd taken out of my hair, she was calm—as she almost always was. As usual, she provided the calm outside the storm of both school and church.

CHAPTER THREE

GOING NATIONWIDE

BY THE TIME I WAS IN HIGH SCHOOL, THE CHURCH WAS SETTING its sights beyond Topeka, sending groups of picketers all over the United States. Westboro's message eventually spread to just about every country in the world—it was so easy, thanks to the Internet and relentless journalists who visited the church regularly to keep the world apprised of WBC's every move.

Initially, we had a calling tree to figure out who could go to which out-of-town pickets: Shirl would call three church members, who would each call three to four other members with the out-of-town picket specifics. The bottom of the tree would report back to the middle three, who were responsible for letting Shirl know by a specific time so she could take care of the logistics. As technology progressed and members became computer savvy, a program was designed for church members to log in and answer "yes" or "no" to a picket request. Once all the responses were submitted, Shirl would decide who would go where. All of this coordination and organization was done in Shirl's house. She delegated a lot of this work to Megan. Increasingly, it was the church members of my generation—especially Ben, Megan, and my uncle Charles—who were the most computer savvy. Just as my parents' generation had gone to law school, many of my cousins studied computer science, while others studied health care. All professions were discussed and approved by church members for their ability to help the church and its cause. We certainly knew that being well versed in computers would help spread our message farther and wider than ever before.

ONE OF THE FIRST MAJOR OUT-OF-TOWN PICKETS WAS ALSO one of the scariest. It was June of 1995—I was twelve—when seven of us packed into Marge's green van and traveled to Golden, Colorado, to picket outside the Coors Brewery. The beer company had just become the latest publicly traded corporation in the country—the twenty-first, to be exact—to extend employee benefits to same-sex couples. The decision had made national news, and the church felt obligated to picket the brewery. I was sent, along with three adults and three other children, for a picket that was sure to be big news and attract a great amount of media coverage. Marge, my aunt Abi, and Jennifer, a member from outside the family, all volunteered. Among the kids were Sara, Jacob, and Jennifer's younger sister Katherine.

Much of the dull drive through western Kansas was spent singing along to Faith Hill and Reba McEntire, who were favorites of my aunts'. I only knew the words to "The Night the Lights Went Out in Georgia," so when that song wasn't on I spent my time crammed between Sara and my cousin playing nonstop games of I Spy. As we crossed into Colorado, my eyes lit up. The beauty and striking immensity of the Rocky Mountains were just outside my window, and a wave of exhilaration overtook me. Living in the flatlands of Kansas, I had rarely gotten the opportunity to see such a majestic landscape.

A bright red Coors sign announced we had reached our destination. I was thrilled to see that mountain ranges would be visible from the picket, and was antsy to get out of the van. I was so captivated that I neglected to pay attention to the enormous crowd waiting for us. (As I got older and out-of-town pickets became more regular, I continued to get excited about going to pickets with beaches and mountains, where I could have a fun vacation while preaching Gramps's gospel.)

Following a police escort, Marge navigated the van through a huge crowd of angry counter-protestors to the picket location outside the brewery. We scrambled out of the van and grabbed our signs and banners, doing our best to ignore the heckling and screaming of the crowd. It was just before two, and the sun was still high in the sky.

"Go home! Go home!" they yelled as I grabbed a red, green, and black TURN OR BURN sign out of the back of the van, one of the less abrasive choices whose meaning, even at that young age, I felt I understood; it became my go-to sign for many pickets to come. Under police protection, we made our way to our designated picketing spot, where I took hold in the middle of our fifteen-foot banner bearing our website's URL, GODHATESFAGS.COM. We made our line among a handful of police officers and hundreds of anti-Westboro activists, who quickly began to surround us on all sides. But, convinced we were God's chosen messengers, we stood tall and unafraid. We were invincible.

"God loves everyone!" someone nearby shouted over the roar of the noisy crowd, starting a chant that quickly spread.

"God hates fags! God hates fag enablers!" responded the WBC adults in their loudest voices and in unison. Catching on, the other kids and I joined in.

"We're here, we're queer, get used to it!" someone else retorted, starting another chant.

"You're here, you're queer, you'll be in hell next year!" Marge screamed back, laughing. We picked up on this new chant with even more enthusiasm.

Through all of the counter-protestors' screams of "fuck you" and "go home," passing cars honked their horns incessantly, and many people flipped us off. A few people even mooned us, evoking a cry of "mooner!" from the first one of us to spot a bare backside—that was our cue to turn our eyes to the ground. No matter the situation, the WBC knew how to prepare for a picket—we had a plan for everything.

After a while some of the crowd started to lose steam and the chanting died down a bit. In a rare quiet moment, I took in the scene. The people there were from all walks of life: different sizes, ages, ethnicities, sexual preferences—the latter made evident by uninhibited kissing in front of us. Some wore bright colors and had wild hairstyles, everything from Mohawks to dreadlocks. Some had more piercings and tattoos than I could count and painted their fingernails black. I thought that was cool—*I could never pull off black polish*, I thought. Likewise the crazy hairstyles. I amused myself thinking just how my family would react if I came home with a Mohawk. The kissing, though, made me squirm, like PDA always did—and not really because they were gay. I felt that way when anybody got too kissy in public.

Some of them, though, were still so infuriated that spit would fly out of their mouths as they shouted. They gestured violently, shaking their fingers hard as they spoke. They all had one thing in common: they were absolutely livid.

I was still silently observing the crowd when I noticed a tall, dark-haired man with a small hoop earring in his right ear standing right behind me. He began to cough; I turned to see that he was skinny and sickly looking, and immediately feared he had AIDS. I was horrified by what I had learned of the disease in church, and assumed I was going to catch it from his coughing.

"He keeps coughing on me!" I yelled to Abi, who was standing next to me singing a WBC-style parody of "Sing" by the Carpenters. She continued to sing against the noise of the crowd in a high falsetto voice. She had promised to watch over me during the picket and I leaned in closer to make sure she heard me. "Make him stop!" I begged, tears now welling in my eyes.

"You'll be fine," she said, as she tossed water on me from her water bottle to clean off what I assumed were AIDS-infested germs. She made a twisted, scornful face at the man, and he backed off for a second, intimidated.

A few moments later, the coughing man began to hit my rear end at a quick, even tempo with his half empty water bottle, which made me feel even more revolted and unnerved. I turned to Abi, who was still singing and completely absorbed in the protest, but said nothing. Tears began streaming down my face. There was nothing I could do. I was helpless, knowing that no one there, not even the police, would be willing to help me.

We gathered up to leave thirty minutes later, accompanied by a singing crowd.

"Na-na-naaa-na. Na-na-naaa-na. Hey, hey, hey. Goodbye!" they cheered in unison. "Na-na-naaa-na. Na-na-naaa-na. Hey, hey, hey. God hates fags," was our rehearsed response.

On our way back to the van, I was shoved backward by someone in the crowd. Knocked flat on my back and still holding my sign with both hands, I screamed, fearing I'd soon be kicked and trampled by the enclosing mob. Two policemen came out of nowhere, grabbed me under each arm, and flung me up with more strength than necessary. They lifted me up with so much force I felt I was momentarily flying through the air. But it all happened so quickly that I was able to shake it off and catch up with the group without falling too far behind.

Making it back to the van, I was praised by everyone for taking the hit without letting go of my sign. No one asked if I was all right, or expressed any concern for me over what had just happened. At that moment, their true intentions showed through. The image of the church was truly what mattered above everything, and everyone, else.

IN ADDITION TO OUR PICKETS, THE CHURCH WAS BEGINNING to gain notoriety for parodies of pop songs. Much the way pickets allowed us to see the world, our sendups of Top 40 songs became an excuse to listen to a lot of popular music, which most of us would have done anyway.

Gramps had started the tradition with simple riffs on Christmas or old-timey songs, like "Grand Old Flag"—which became "Filthy Flag," in his version—and "I'm Proud to Be an American," which became "I'm Ashamed to Be an American":

I'm ashamed to be an American, where the fags can freely
    roam
They spread their filth around this land, every pervert calls
    it home
So I'll gladly stand up—with a picket sign —and proclaim
    God's word today
Cuz there ain't no doubt about this land—God hates the USA.

Music had always been a big part of my life; my dad played the piano every night, practicing for Sunday services, and Sara and I both sang in the school choir. In high school, we performed a duet of the Bette Midler song "The Rose," and people showed up just to see it. Mostly because Sara is a really good singer, but I wasn't so bad myself. I harmonized well with her. So when it came to performing song parodies for the church, we tended to be front and center.

Gran was good at music—she had a great singing voice, and had even sung at her own wedding. It became a friendly competition among all of us to see who could belt out a song the loudest and proudest; Shirl and Marge both thought themselves the best singers on the planet, but my aunt Abi had the most pitch-perfect voice. Sara and I were the reigning champs at harmonizing. In general, singing livened up a picket, which could get monotonous after an hour of standing with huge signs in our hands, getting yelled at (or worse) by people driving by.

At Christmas, the church's spin on carols became our own version of a holiday tradition. We didn't celebrate the actual holiday, because as Gramps said, it was a bastardized, pagan celebration of idolatry that had no actual basis in the Bible. But we put our stamp on the season with a hymnal of fire-and-brimstone carols. On Christmas Eve, we would picket churches having candlelight services; we'd stay out until midnight, singing songs like "Silent Night":

Silent night, awful night
You have no peace
You're full of fright
God's righteous anger is close and near
His hate for this nation is painfully clear

Behold the wrath of the lamb
Behold the wrath of the lamb.

As the church became more well known after 9/11, and our mission expanded to excoriating America as a whole, church leaders decided we'd take mainstream pop idols and turn them upside down.

WHEN MICHAEL JACKSON DIED, WE CAME OUT WITH A VERSION of "We Are the World" called "God Hates the World." When *Shrek* was popular, I suggested doing a take on "Holding Out for a Hero," an '80s song that regained popularity with its inclusion in the animated movie. My aunt Marge, whose quick wit made her a natural at writing pointed lyrics, quickly came up with "There Are No Heroes"—and the credit for thinking of it eventually went to Sara, much to my chagrin. Every time we watched a movie, we would be on alert for songs we could use to our advantage. It became a game of sorts. But more than that, it was a fun family activity.

Those song parodies were one of the things I missed the most when I left the church. I wish I could go back and sing with my cousins and aunts and uncles again, even if I didn't always believe in the words I was singing. To be honest, I didn't really think too hard about what they meant. I knew they echoed the message we were charged to bring to the world, and that was really all that mattered.

THE SEEDS OF DOUBT REALLY SPROUTED IN ME IN EARNEST AT seventeen, in 2000, on a road trip with my family. "What would we talk about if we didn't talk about picketing?" Sara chirped in the car while we were en route to a picket, an overnight's drive from Topeka. "Don't even think that way," my dad chided her, leaving the discussion at that.

The brief exchange came back to haunt me that night as I lay in my Motel 6 bed next to Sara. *Why do our lives have to revolve around picketing?* I wondered as I drifted off to sleep. *Why do our "loving" family activities have to revolve around conflict and hate?*

As I grew into my teenage years, the church became gradually even more condemning of the outside world—and strict and unforgiving with even its own members. My own parents began to treat us more harshly, which was not their traditional style.

But my doubts took root slowly. I was afraid to question what I had been raised to believe. I couldn't even begin to picture what life would be like outside of the church. We were living the good life, I was told constantly. For a long time, I thought I was.

ONE OF MY FAVORITE THINGS ABOUT MY CHILDHOOD WAS how much I got to travel, which was way more than most kids from Topeka did. In part—and increasingly as I got older—this was because we were picketing all over the country. But a little-known secret about the church was that we would tailor our pickets to places we wanted to visit anyway. Nobody really said it out loud, of course, but it was understood that when we traveled some distance to represent the church, we had also earned a little time off for recreation. My parents, Sara, Ben, and I were always happy to get in some sightseeing. If you look through my old photo albums, you'll see page after page of my vacation photos, often pictures of us holding picket signs, which I've scrupulously augmented with cheery stickers and brightly colored markers adding commentary about silly things that happened at the time. To an outsider, I realize this might look really bizarre: A typical young girl's album—complete with "i"s dotted with hearts—crossed with a decades-long chronicle of gay-bashing.

When I was in grade school, there had been a few wholesome family trips we could take without picketing at all that wouldn't arouse condemnation from Shirl. One of them was our every-other-year pilgrimage to Branson, Missouri, the Christian-friendly town with lots of musicals and amusement parks, but no alcohol. We'd go on a road trip to Yellowstone National Park and then the next year to Branson, where we once saw an Osmond Brothers concert Sara and I loved so much we led a standing ovation at the end. Religion didn't always have to be an overt part of those trips, at least not until the rules of the church began to get more stringent.

By the time I was in my teens, every trip had to have a church-affiliated reason for existence. We wanted to go to Hawaii, so we planned in a day of general picketing in Honolulu, in front of a couple of churches and on Punchbowl Street, chosen for its foot traffic. After those pickets—which I remember mainly for their laid-back feeling, as passersby seemed much less confrontational than on the mainland—we were free to go to the beach without fear of reprisal when we got back. Years later, my brother Ben honeymooned in Hawaii, where he and his new wife made sure to picket for a few scant minutes—and have photographic evidence of it to show around to the family afterward. When we went to Cocoa Beach in Florida we took a few signs, whipped them out on the beach, and snapped a couple of photos to prove we'd been doing right by the church edicts. For the trip to Puerto Rico—my last vacation with my family before I left the church—we packed shirts that said PriestsRapeBoys.com, GodHatesFags.com, and GodHatesAmerica.com, and pulled them out on the side of the road in front of a beautiful church and took a few pictures so we could say we picketed in Puerto Rico.

Shirl, of course, maintained a literally holier-than-thou attitude; her favorite saying about vacations was, "I would never travel anywhere I couldn't picket." She seemed totally incapable of having fun, and it was hard to imagine her traveling anywhere and being interested in anything other than harassing people on the street. She was also nursing an unfounded paranoia about any of us going outside the country, afraid the government would persecute us and refuse to let us back in. My aunt Rachel once had the chance to go on vacation with her husband, Charles, to an island outside the US, and Shirl shut it down quickly. But while Shirl's fears about international trips might have been unfounded, there was a danger closer to home that we hadn't anticipated. People's anger toward us was becoming more aggressive, with violence erupting in a way that it never had before.

One day when I was a teenager, as we picketed outside the Washburn Law School, a woman drove her pickup truck directly at us, swerving at the last minute. We scattered, running for safety. Later we sued, but she was found not guilty due to temporary insanity. Still, within the church, this was seen as a victory for us—maybe not legally, but the fact that we'd had that much of an impact on someone. It also marked the beginning of a darker turn for Westboro pickets, in which our physical safety began to be more of a concern—not that it ever stopped Gramps or Shirl from putting us all out there on the picket line.

By that time, our picketing ministry was well established; we had even sent a group to Washington, DC, in January 1993 to picket the AIDS quilt, which had gotten us onto the national radar. Thanks to Shirl's meticulous spreadsheets, we had groups organized to go out every day of the year in Topeka—no exceptions. And whether or not there was an out-of-town picket, we always made sure there was a group protesting in Topeka as well. One of our highest-profile local targets had recently become the Vintage restaurant, which would become one of the most notorious WBC protest sites in the church's history. Gramps always liked to refer to a picket as "an unforgettable experience," but this one took it to another level: the hospital.

The Vintage was one of the nicest restaurants in town, a place where local and visiting politicians would often have meetings over meals. When Gramps got wind of its manager, Sharon York, being appointed to a gay and lesbian council in town, the place immediately went on our weekly picket list. I was told the reason we were picketing was because the manager was a lesbian, but I still didn't really know what that meant; I just assumed she was a bad person, that gay people were disgusting and a terrible influence and dangerous to be around kids. As an extra bonus, the Vintage was just down the street from a church Gramps didn't like, which meant we could kill two birds with one stone and spread our picket out over a couple of blocks.

Unlike a lot of people we picketed, who basically resigned themselves to ignoring us as the pickets became a part of their everyday lives, this particular target didn't take the protest lying down. For weeks, as we stood outside with our signs, Sharon York and the cooks would come outside for smoke breaks, giving us the finger and yelling at us to go home. Their anger just made Gramps's resolve stronger. The pickets became larger; the Vintage staff got more riled up. The owner, Jerry Berger, began coming outside when we showed up, asking us to leave because our presence there was hurting business. Gramps and Shirl were unmoved and even a little amused by this.

When we didn't back down, Berger decided to take matters into his own hands. It all came to a head one day that lives in infamy in our family's history, a day the Phelpses still refer to as "the Vintage Massacre."

On the evening of March 26, 1993, when our picket showed up around five thirty, Berger emerged from the restaurant's front door with a small group of big, burly men. Much to Gramps's initial glee, Berger had actually gone so far as to hire security to guard the Vintage against us. We all assumed they'd stay in front of the restaurant, but they quickly crossed the parking lot and began walking along the picket line. My uncle Chris was in charge of recording that day—we always tried to record, in case we needed to use anything in court later—and he got the video camera rolling right away. One of the big men smacked the camcorder out of his hand, and it smashed on the ground. Another pushed my uncle Tim, who pushed back; soon Tim was on the ground being kicked by two of the men. "Stop! You'll kill him!" one of my aunts yelled at them. Soon it was a full-on melee, with the men in our group being pummeled by Berger's thugs while Gran yelled at the WBC women to run, and dialed 911. Someone grabbed a camera out of my sister Sharon's hand as she snapped pictures of the violence; she kicked at him and grabbed it back. The men didn't hurt Gramps, though; Berger stood next to him while the violence went on, asking him how it felt to see people he loved being hurt. Finally, the police and ambulances arrived; several of my uncles, Ben, and Sharon went to the hospital. Ben and Tim were injured the most; they were taken away on stretchers with neck braces on. Years later Ben still complained of back and neck pain. Uncle Tim had gotten his head kicked in. He still has neck issues.

From then on, we've picketed at that location every day, and every March 26 is our memorial for the Vintage Massacre—including a huge picket at the Vintage. Sharon York was eventually fired from the restaurant because Jerry Berger said we'd made it impossible to keep her employed there. It was a hard-won victory for Westboro; we used the photo evidence from that night on our signs for years afterward to demonstrate how—just like Jesus—our family members had been cruelly beaten for their beliefs. VINTAGE THUGS BEAT KIDS, our signs read.

NEWS STORIES ABOUT THE DUSTUP HELPED RAISE THE PROFILE of our picketing ministry, already getting increasingly better known. We had attracted attention for our regular presence at Gage Park, around Topeka, and at the occasional out-of-state picket. Now, as we began to garner more media attention, we began to think more about how to play up to the cameras that showed up at our pickets. There weren't many teenagers in America who spent slumber parties practicing how to talk to the media on the topic of God hating gay people and how America is doomed—but Megan and I did, even tape recording ourselves acting the parts of interviewer and interviewee.

On summer nights, we would do this during sleepovers at various relatives' houses. All the aunts and uncles were happy to host a slumber party now and then, although Uncle Tim and Aunt Lee Ann's house was a special favorite because of Tim's willingness to play with us. Uncle Tim—tall, redheaded, and athletic—would dress all in black and stalk us in our conjoined backyards in a game we called "Ninja," much to our delight.

He would sing and dance to pop songs with us. Elton John was one of his favorite singers. I always wondered why it was collectively deemed OK for him to like a musician who was so obviously gay, but I never dared to say this out loud.

Later, lying side by side on the living-room rug after everyone had gone to bed, we liked to imagine in whispers what life would be like when we grew up. I would curl up in my gray sleeping bag, and Megan would make a bed out of her favorite Little Mermaid blanket. We figured we would live together, since we were never going to get married to anyone. So we meticulously planned out our dream house, complete with black and white checkered floors, that we would live in together while we waited for the apocalypse.

We also wrote practice scripts for getting asked out by boys; it happened occasionally, and we would tell them how disgusting and ugly we were, and that no one would ever find any part of us attractive. When one boy asked me to go to the movies with him, I originally planned to tell him I couldn't because I had to help paint my brother's house—which was the truth. I knew Megan and I could come up with a better response, though, and we painstakingly crafted the perfect comeback: "I'm sorry, but my cultural diversity and religious background have taught me that engaging in such behavior would be detrimental to my spiritual growth and eternal prospects. In other words, I don't date." (Yes, much smoother than the "painting my brother's house" excuse.)

Boys were so forbidden to us that dating never even crossed my mind. It simply wasn't part of who we were. "Avoid the appearance of evil" was the dictate from my family. If we were dating a boy, we were doing it out of lust, which was a sin; there could be no actual love or genuine feelings involved. Matthew 5:28: "But I say unto you, That whosoever looketh on a woman to lust after her hath committed adultery with her already in his heart." Two young people who were dating actually hated each other, we were taught, because both of them wouldn't tell the other the truth about what God required: to serve and obey Him. And to obey Him meant one man and one woman in marriage, nothing else, ever. Hand-holding, kissing, or anything else outside the marital bed was unthinkable. None of us ever talked about sex, even among ourselves, the older kids; no one ever mentioned wanting to date. The only sex education I'd ever gotten had come from a video they showed in my fifth grade class. You'd think I would have at least secretly been interested in the subject like seemingly everyone else in high school, but I really wasn't. Kids would make sexual references that I never got; I simply knew they were perverted, as we always called it. I understood that my role was different, a higher purpose.

It was a known thing at school that the Phelps girls were not allowed to date or even talk to boys in any way outside of school-related topics. This, of course, was irresistible to some of them. One guy named Louis used to like to tease me. During a class, he'd say quietly, "Let's go to the bathroom, Libby. I'll meet you in the bathroom." He'd reach out and touch my arm or my leg, which made me jump. I didn't like that, and I didn't think it was charming—I just thought it was inappropriate.

On volleyball game days, we sometimes had to wear dresses; I would wear a longer skirt than the other girls usually did, so I wouldn't draw too much attention to myself. I was wearing this outfit one afternoon, walking down the hallway between classes, when someone tripped me. I fell, desperately trying to keep my skirt from flying up and scattering my books all over the hallway. I looked around as I got up, but I couldn't see who'd done it—only that lots of kids were laughing about it. I heard Gramps's voice in my head as I gathered up my books, dripping with humiliation: "God'll get 'em for what they did to you." This was his refrain whenever any of the kids would come home with a story about being bullied for being from Westboro. We were supposed to wear it as a badge of honor. I didn't get it as bad as some, because I was pretty big for my age, but I still got it occasionally. At home, my mom would always try to push these incidents under the rug. "Oh, it's not that big of a deal," she'd say, trying to minimize the trauma.

STILL, WHILE I DIDN'T HAVE ANY INTEREST IN BOYS AT SCHOOL, I did wonder how the older people in the church had ever found their spouses to begin with. How had they been allowed to be attracted to another person, to show their emotions? I never got up the courage to ask any of the adults about this, for fear of being mocked or chastised.

When my older brother began dating the woman who is now his wife, he had to be chaperoned at all times, sometimes with cousins as young as six or seven. I'm not sure why anyone thought the presence of a child that young would maintain order or propriety, but that was the rule: There had to be someone else there, even if that someone else was in first grade.

But for a church that stringently maintained rules about one man and one woman in marriage, there were a surprising number of scandalous episodes involving affairs and, several times, miscarriages that resulted from them.

WHEN I WAS THIRTEEN, MY AUNT MARGE HAD A TRYST WITH one of the rare outsiders who'd started coming to the church. His name was George, and he began coming to services with his wife, Cindy, who'd met another aunt of mine, Rachel, through their work at the courthouse in the Child in Need of Care (CINC) department, where Rachel worked when she wasn't at Phelps-Chartered. They were going to become church members.

But things fell apart between the couple when Cindy found out about her husband and Marge. She divorced him and left the church, scandalously scrawling THIS IS BULLSHIT in the Bible Gramps had given her.

It wasn't long after that we learned that Marge was pregnant, and we found this out because she had been ordered—by Gramps or Shirl, most likely—to confess to it in front of the entire congregation. George was in church the morning she did it, and I remember seeing him sitting with his head bowed way down, clutching his Bible with one hand and holding his head with the other.

Marge's adopted son Jacob, who was twelve at the time, began crying as she explained that she had become pregnant because of an illicit affair with George. "You had sex with him?" he yelled at her through his tears, in front of everyone. Jacob had always been kind of slow for his age. They would never admit there was anything wrong with him, though, or anyone else in the church; it simply wasn't conceivable that there could be anything wrong with God's chosen ones. (My cousin Zach, who left the church a couple of years ago, was finally diagnosed with severe bipolar disorder.)

Later that day, when Jacob and I were walking to a picket at the corner of 17th and Gage, he asked me worriedly, "Do you think my mom is going to hell?" "I dunno," I said. "I don't think anybody knows, but she's certainly not behaving herself."

Soon after that announcement, George disappeared. We were told it was because he was a nonbeliever who'd never be one of God's elect, though it seemed more likely that he couldn't handle the stress and scrutiny of Marge's pregnancy shaming.

When she was about eight months pregnant, Marge got sick. She went into Gran's room and lay down on the couch, telling my other aunts that the baby hadn't moved in a few days. They took her to the hospital, and she gave birth to a stillborn baby girl. My aunt Rachel told me, "The doctors say maybe the umbilical cord wrapped around its neck, but we all know what really happened—God did it." Marge herself joined in the chorus, telling the congregation on the Sunday after the stillbirth, "This is God's judgment on me."

But the baby had not been left at the hospital, we discovered. One afternoon, Jacob took me into Gran's bathroom, where alongside the washer and dryer they had a large meat freezer. He opened it and showed me a Styrofoam cooler sitting on top of the meat. Inside was Marge's baby, tiny and bluish; she probably weighed four pounds, with two of those pounds settled in her chubby cheeks. We stared at her silently. I had never seen a dead body before, and I doubt he had either. Jacob reached in and put his teddy bear on top of her and closed the top.

The baby was buried in the yard, near the volleyball court, where there was a small patch of open grass. Marge named her Hannah. They had a family funeral and buried her with a tiny stone on top, bearing no name at all. Later, they would bury another stillborn baby—this one belonging to Shirl, who named her dead son Jeremiah. Even though I never got the opportunity to meet these sweet babies, tears streamed down my face during both funerals. Losing a baby is horrible. During these moments both Marge and Shirl were far from their hate-spewing selves. I felt sorry for them—what a terrible thing to go through.

THESE WERE SECRETS THAT WERE KEPT ON LOCKDOWN WITHIN the family, but we weren't supposed to talk about the church at all when we were out in the world—other than at a picket— or at school. Even though I had grown up being prepared to be demonized, marginalized, and hated by my classmates, I expected to be treated like anyone else by the students and, more importantly, by the teachers, who were supposed to be fair. For the most part, I wasn't actively picked on by the other kids. They would mostly just ask questions: "Why do you guys do that?" When people were mean to me, I could generally shrug it off. I joined the volleyball team, and I did track; I was a horrible runner, but I could throw the shot put fairly well. Being good at something athletic made it much easier to fit in and avoid bullying. There were always a few people who would single me out, though. One girl, whom I had never spoken to in my life, would be sure to say, "I hate that girl," every time I walked past her. But Sara, who was more sensitive than me and didn't have the benefit of being into sports (other than tennis) got it worse than I did.

ONE DAY, THE TWO OF US WERE WALKING BACK INTO SCHOOL after having left to get lunch. As we crossed through the science building to get to another classroom on the other side, we caught sight of a girl called Destinee, who was glaring in our direction.

"I don't like that girl," Sara muttered to me. Destinee whipped around.

"What did you just say?" She walked up to my sister and slapped her. Stunned, Sara recoiled, but I was furious. I ran over in front of Destinee, grabbed her forearms, and twisted them back. We wrestled for a minute until my science teacher, Mr. Rupp, broke it up, sending all of us to the principal's office.

And who should come to the office to meet us? Not our parents but Shirl, who was always in charge of this kind of thing.

"Stay calm," she commanded us as we sat outside the office with her. "Just tell them what happened. You didn't do anything wrong." We all had to go in and tell our sides of the story.

Afterward, I headed to choir practice as usual, and a girl named Caitlin caught up with me in the hallway. She had always been very kind to me.

"What happened?" she said. "Everyone's talking." I filled her in, but as I was talking Destinee walked by us, uncomfortably close. I got shaky; I was afraid she was going to hit me. She ultimately got suspended for hitting Sara.

Right after the meeting, I had to rush to the theater to try on my costume for *The Sound of Music*, where I was playing—what else—a nun. Backstage in the costume closet, I tried not to cry, but I clearly looked upset. Ashley, a fellow nun, looked concerned.

"Did a boy break up with you?" she asked. I half laughed. "You know I don't date!" I said. That was what most everyone my age worried about, though. I wasn't allowed to even think about it, although my friend Antwayn regularly told me he had a crush on me. I always believed he was gay—he certainly seemed that way to me, anyway—but it didn't mean I was rude to him. We were instructed to be nice to everyone when we were out in the world. "You never know how your message is going to fall in their hearts," we were told by Gramps. So unfailing friendliness—even when we were holding a sign that preached hate—was our bylaw.

AND TO BE FAIR, WE DID HOLD SIGNS *NEAR* SCHOOL, ALTHOUGH never on school grounds (that would have violated Gramps's policy of not talking about Westboro there). At Topeka West, we held a weekly picket across the street from the school parking lot, so all the kids coming and going could see the signs. Because I wasn't technically in school, it was OK for me to talk to kids about Westboro and religion. Some were curious; one guy named Joe came over once and asked me what the signs were about. I told him we were picketing because there was a Gay Student Alliance, and that students were at an impressionable age and needed to see our signs to know that gay support groups were wrong. He didn't say much about what he believed one way or another; I got the sense he'd been dared by his friends to come up to us. Other kids weren't so reserved. Some would save the parts of the school lunch they didn't want—usually the vegetables—and throw them at us out of car windows as they were pulling away.

MORE WORRISOME THAN HATE FROM FELLOW STUDENTS WAS when teachers would turn against us. I was a good student; I worked hard to maintain a perfect GPA so I could get a scholarship to Washburn University, as I'd long dreamed.

Honors English in my junior year was taught by Mrs. Wilson. I could tell straightaway that she didn't like me, so I tried to fly under the radar. One day, our assignment was to read "Sinners in the Hands of an Angry God," the sermon by Jonathan Edwards that describes people going to hell. It was the basis for many of Gramps's own sermons. I stayed silent during that class discussion, because I feared the reaction from my classmates; I didn't want anyone claiming I had talked about religion.

I kept getting Cs in her class despite feeling sure I'd done the work right. I would write a paper and have my mom and my aunts read it, go into class feeling good, and get a middling grade. She seemed to fairly obviously not like me, and I knew she was a Unitarian—they're the ones who are famously tolerant of gays in the church—so I strongly suspected it had to do with the church. I didn't know who to talk to about it; all I wanted to do at school was to go about my business without being noticed, get good grades, and not mention the church. But I knew those Cs would hurt my chances of going to college and venturing further away from my family.

I finally told Ben, who'd had Mrs. Wilson for a teacher too, what was going on. The class syllabus was the same as it had been back when he was a student, eight years earlier, so he gave me one of his A-grade papers, and I copied it word for word—something I'd never have done otherwise, but we agreed we wanted to test out my theory. Again, she gave me a C.

I confessed to my parents what we'd done, and my dad called my teacher that night. "You know what you're doing, and you're not going to get away with it!" I could hear him from the next room. As I've mentioned, he gets pretty scary when he gets mad. Even though his anger was aimed at her and not me, I was incredibly nervous. Through the right channels, I got my grade changed to not harm my GPA.

THERE WERE OTHER INSTANCES WHEN TEACHERS TREATED ME differently for being from WBC. I always loved singing, and in high school I wanted to be a part of Singers, the top choral group in the school. But I had been warned about the teacher, Mrs. Epoch, by my family. I had, in fact, been told that she was evil and to stay away from her. This likely meant that she had at some point spoken publicly against the church. As it turned out, she did seem to harbor a grudge against me. She told me I couldn't be in the group—until I got a perfect score from the audition judges, which even she couldn't refute.

THEN THERE WAS SEMINAR, A STUDY HALL CLASS WHERE WE got an A just for showing up every day. We could arrange to get help from other teachers during the period, which I usually did. I could tell the teacher didn't like me, so I arranged to be gone as much as possible. Later in the day, a girl named Chrissy, who was a cheerleader, pulled me aside. "I can't believe what she was saying about you," she told me. Apparently after I'd left class, the teacher had remarked, "I wish I had the guts to tell her what I think about her. The nerve of her, picketing in front of the school every week." I got a B in that class, despite its being an easy A. Again, going through the right channels, I was able to stay in this mandatory class without it affecting my GPA.

THERE WERE, HOWEVER, SOME TEACHERS WHO LOOKED AT US as individuals rather than extensions of the church. Mr. Perry taught Current Issues and was always fair and understanding when my family came up. One of our favorite English teachers,

Mr. Newbery, encouraged us to keep notebooks and journals of our thoughts. He would read them periodically and leave us notes in the margins. Later, his work with Megan and Grace would help them find the strength to leave the church.

FIVE YEARS AFTER THE VINTAGE, THERE WAS ANOTHER TURNING point for us, in the form of a major news story about a young man in Wyoming who had been killed for being gay. One Sunday after church, I heard a conversation among my aunts and uncles about a college student named Matthew Shepard, who had been "trolling for sex" and gotten mixed up with the wrong guys. God, they said, had planned for him to run into the two men who tortured him and left him tied to a fence to die. This was apt punishment, we kids were told, for his sin of being a fag. I felt a creeping sense of disbelief that we were all celebrating such a grisly murder, but the more I talked to my cousins about it, the more Gramps's views were reinforced for me: He was a disgusting, filthy fag and shouldn't have been doing what he did.

The church's views were, as usual, in direct contrast to what was being said about the killing in the media, which was that Shepard had been the innocent target of a despicable hate crime—when, in reality, he was anything but innocent because he'd been looking for immoral sex, the church said. As Gramps told us on so many occasions, anyone outside our church was so deluded and defiled they had no idea what the real story was.

He saw this incident as a prime opportunity for some higher-profile picketing, and organized a group to drive to Shepard's funeral in Casper, Wyoming. A MATT IN HELL sign was created for the occasion, with a cutout of the young man's head emblazoned with an upside-down pink triangle: the sign of the gay rights movement, turned upside down. Gramps would hold that one, as well as another one targeted to calls for more hate crime legislation: NO SPECIAL LAWS FOR FAGS.

At the picket, which we excitedly watched on the national news, Gramps wore his traditional windbreaker and cowboy hat, brandishing his signs and laughing. "You should have seen all those fags," he would tell us later, chortling. (Years later when a play, *The Laramie Project,* was written about Shepard's life, we would picket that too. Supporters of Shepard showed up at the picket, dressed as angels with huge sheet-covered white wings that effectively blocked our group from being seen by anyone attending the show. It was a pretty effective stunt—and we knew all about those.)

On the way home from the funeral, my uncle Charles got into a car accident on the highway and flipped his jeep. Nobody was hurt, thankfully. But I wondered why God would let such a thing happen to a group of His chosen people on their way to spread His word.

Looking back on it today, I feel like it was glaringly wrong to picket somebody's funeral. But I didn't think that then. I just thought—like we all did, like we'd been told—that we were there to warn the people who were alive. That they should repent. The Westboro rationale for everything.

When I think now of the way that boy died, tied up on that post, I feel awful. But at the time, I didn't think it was that big a deal—or maybe I didn't think about it that much, period. Now I'm a mother, and all I can think is what if that happened to my son; what if somebody tied him up and left him to die?

IN THE DAYS FOLLOWING THE SHEPARD PICKET, THE CHURCH'S address had been made public and we were seeing a steep increase in hate mail. In Gramps's eyes, business was better than ever—people were angrier with us than they'd ever been before. It was the first time the church had ever publicly targeted a person's funeral, and the outrage was pouring in every day.

One of my after-school chores was to go to Gran and Gramps's house and help out with whatever they needed, which included getting the mail. The stack of letters in the mailbox usually included at least one or two handwritten notes telling them off.

My favorite part, though, was arriving in Gran's kitchen after school, taking a seat at one of the tall chairs in the kitchen, and talking about life with her as she puttered around. One afternoon she remembered she needed to get the mail, and I stopped her, jumping out of my chair and jogging through the church sanctuary, through the green office, and out the double doors to the front of the church with its green and white striped canopy. Smiling all the way. We were always supposed to be smiling, but I actually felt like doing it when I was at Gran and Gramps's place. Down the sidewalk a short distance was the mailbox, next to the church marquee, creepily sporting a bullet hole someone had recently put in it. I grabbed the stack of mail and headed into the fireplace room where Gran spent a lot of her downtime. It was more comfortable to sit on the couch in there, so I plopped down and yelled into the pantry to ask if I could open the mail. Gran, who was organizing bottles of Diet Pepsi and cans of soup, said yes. Sitting on the couch, I thumbed through the mail, putting aside junk mailers. I spotted a handwritten letter—my favorite—and wanted to open it. I loved reading the letters. Most of the time they were from people who disagreed with or outright hated us. But there were a few, especially in the early years, that were supportive. I was always curious about what others had to say.

This one was a note card with the words EAT SHIT AND DIE written inside. Folded inside the card was a piece of toilet paper with a streak of brown on it. My excitement turned to shock. I don't know which was more upsetting, seeing the word "shit" or the thing itself. I sat quietly for a couple of minutes, wondering what in the world was wrong with this person that they'd want to do something like this. It was, I concluded, just more verification of everything we'd been told about how people would treat us for preaching the truth. Closing the card, I went to Gran in the kitchen and told her about it.

"I'm so sorry you had to see that," Gran consoled me as I washed my hands for the eighth time. She kept apologizing. She seemed unfazed, like this was the kind of thing she expected or dealt with all the time. I told her not to look at it, and when I had her OK I threw it away—though I wondered if one of our lawyers could somehow figure out who'd done it from the stool sample. "It's not that easy," said Gran, smiling anyway. Always smiling.

THE NEXT SUMMER, BEFORE MY SENIOR YEAR OF HIGH SCHOOL, I woke up on a hot summer day with a stomachache. I knew I wasn't supposed to complain—this was seen as being selfish instead of focusing on helping the church, which meant helping God—but while I was in the backyard watching my mom's day care kids with her, I couldn't help it and told her about the weird, stabbing sensation in my middle. As usual, she brushed it off; I think she always hoped if she didn't pay attention to our complaints they'd just go away. So I just pushed through the pain until it was time to go to the noon pickets.

I was responsible for picking up Tim and Lee Ann's kids and transporting them to the midday pickets. The pickets today were at our regular daily spots, 17th and Gage—because St. David's Episcopal Church was located there, and they had been the most vocal against WBC ministry in the beginning when we started out just picketing Gage Park and the Vintage. Moving slower than usual, I got into my white Corolla and got the kids. We parked on the side of the road, a block away from 17th and Gage, got out, walked to the white-sign truck, and waited our turn to pull our signs out of the truck bed. I opted against taking one of the big signs, as I normally would have. I took a little sign instead, in hopes of decreasing the stress the heavy weight put on my body. We walked the block to the picketing intersection and turned our signs in sync with the changing traffic lights, making sure everyone passing would see. I stood by Gramps.

"I can't think of a better thing to be doing on a nice day like today than having a nice picket with my loved ones, don't you agree?" he said, smiling at me. He had his usual cowboy hat and windbreaker on, and he was wielding his favorite GOD HATES FAGS sign.

"Yep!" I agreed, bending forward slightly because of the pain in my stomach. I kept a big smile on my face so Gramps wouldn't suspect anything was wrong.

"We gotta keep in the faces of these godforsaken false prophets masquerading as preachers," Gramps said, which was what he always said. "Spreading the big Arminian lie that God loves everyone. They're responsible for all these people headed straight to hell in a faggot's handbasket. You know that, right, hon?"

"Yep," I said, nodding, sweating. I looked up at the traffic light to make sure my sign was oriented perpendicular to oncoming traffic.

"Good," said Gramps. "It's our duty to prophesy against these so-called prophets. You ever heard of Ezekiel

13? That passage tells us to prophesy against them; it's our duty."

Bending forward in even more pain, I wasn't sure how to respond. What did he want me to say? Was I even supposed to say anything? Or just listen to him? Maybe he was just practicing for his upcoming Sunday sermon.

"Are you doing OK, lovebug?" said Gramps. "You don't look like you feel very well."

"My stomach hurts really bad," I admitted. "I think I'm going to throw up."

"Maybe you need to go home," he said.

"But I have to take Tim's kids to the next picket," I said. By now my stomach was really killing me, but by golly, I was going to do my duty and get those kids to the next picket.

"I'm sure they can walk the three blocks there," said Gramps with a laugh. "Go on home."

"OK," I said, "I'm going to go, then." Picking up my sign, I walked toward the truck with tears in my eyes—partly because of the twisting pain in my stomach, but also because I'd failed in my duty to serve God and His people. Would Gramps think I was weak? Would he think I didn't deserve the responsibility I'd been given to take the kids to the pickets?

I put my sign away and drove the two blocks back to my house. Plodding up the stairs to my pink-carpeted bedroom, I lay down on my bed and curled up into a ball. Eventually, my mother appeared in the doorway.

"Are you OK?" she said. "Why aren't you at the picket?"

"Help," I moaned, unable to pretend anymore. "It hurts so bad I can barely move."

I must have really looked awful, because she decided to take me to the emergency room. But I didn't know if I could get up. I'd never felt pain like this before. Along with the pain came a crippling sense of guilt. I didn't want to interrupt everyone's day, and I certainly didn't want to be the center of attention. What if the church decided that my heart wasn't in the right place, so God was punishing me by giving me this awful pain? Would I be admonished for whatever sins had caused the illness? I found myself crying again.

"Come on," my mom said. "I'll help you."

Small as she was, she supported my weight as I got off the bed and limped downstairs to the garage. She drove to the Topeka hospital's emergency room while I sat next to her in the front passenger seat, moaning in pain. For some reason the moaning seemed to help ease the pain. Maybe it was all in my mind, but the vibration from moaning felt like it helped lessen the pain in my internal organs.

The ER waiting room was bustling, and my mom checked me in. "There's going to be a wait," said the heavyset nurse on duty. "We're busy today."

Ugh, I thought, sinking onto the nearest chair and putting my hands on my stomach. I overheard the staff talking about another patient. "He comes in all the time, I'm sure there's nothing wrong with him, as usual," one nurse said to another. I got up and bolted for the restroom, making it just in time before I threw up. I was getting worse. Why wouldn't they take me back? I felt like I was going to die.

"David, come on back," they called to the man they'd been talking about earlier. *Seriously?* I grumbled to myself. *The guy who comes in all the time with nothing ever wrong with him gets to go back before me?* I continued to wait for what felt like hours, bent over in my chair with my arms around my middle. Finally, they called me back; I told the nurse I had a terrible stomachache, the worst I could ever remember.

He gave me a hospital gown and told me to put it on, then left the room. I didn't know how to put on a hospital gown. I'd never needed to wear one before today. I decided to leave it open in the front, because they needed to get to my stomach. The nurse came back in and told me with a smile that I had put the gown on backward. When he gave me another, I overlapped the two; I didn't want to be lying around with my naked rear end immodestly showing out the back of the gown.

The nurse reappeared, and had me lie down on the exam table. He pushed down on my lower right abdominal area and I screamed in pain; I hadn't thought anything could feel worse than my stomach already did, but this was worse.

"I think you might have appendicitis," he said, "but we'll need to do further testing before we decide what to do. Until then I'll give you some medicine for the pain. I'm going to need you to sign a few papers approving the medicine and testing," he said, handing my mom some forms. To my relief, she didn't hesitate after looking them over, and signed them.

Minutes later, I was mercifully numbed with pain medication, and wheeled on my hospital bed to get an MRI. I was met with a smile from the MRI technician, a good-looking young gentleman with dark hair in his early twenties. He explained that he would be putting me in a tube and that I was to lie still while the machine worked. I was transferred to the MRI table, and as half of my body entered the machine, I sat up and threw up all over myself and the MRI machine. I was too weak and in too much pain to feel very embarrassed, but I apologized out of habit. He was very sympathetic, and smiled at me, and told me it was fine. He cleaned it all up, then got me back in position. After the MRI was completed, I was wheeled back to my room. Shortly afterward, Dr. Hamilton, the surgeon, came in. I smiled, again out of habit more than anything else.

"I know you must be in a lot of pain if you're smiling when the surgeon comes in!" he joked. I tried to laugh through the pain.

"She has pretty severe appendicitis," the doctor told my mother. "Close to bursting, but it hasn't yet. We need to get her into surgery as soon as possible to remove it."

Surgery! I turned to my mom, wide-eyed. She smiled gently at me.

"It will be all right," she said. I didn't know if it would be. This was a really big deal. What had I done wrong that had put me here?

"What are they going to do?" I asked my mother.

"I'm sure they'll walk you through everything," she said. "I'll be with you until you go in."

We watched television for a few minutes to get our minds off the upcoming operation. By this point, it was ten at night, well past my bedtime, and I was exhausted.

Finally, they came to get me, stopping halfway down the hallway to tell my mom she couldn't come any further.

"I love you," she said to me, kissing me on the forehead. It was the only time I could remember her giving me a kiss. I imagine she'd done it when I was a baby, but never after that.

I was scared, but I lay back and tried to relax as they continued wheeling me in. The anesthesiologist put a mask over my nose and mouth and asked me to count back from 100. Destiny's Child's "Say My Name" was playing in the background, I was humming along, then began to count down, 100, 99, 98, 97, 96, 95—I was out.

I woke up to the sight of my mom's face beside my bed, and a nurse beside her. "I can't believe you didn't wake up and ask for any pain medicine," the nurse said. "That's amazing!" Compared to the way I'd felt before the surgery, this was nothing.

I smiled at my mom as my vitals were taken. I felt so much better. "Let me know if you start having pain and need pain medicine," the nurse told me.

Soon, my aunts and uncles started calling to check up on me and sending get-well cards and flowers and stuffed animals. I had been so afraid I would be shunned for getting sick, but it seemed like I had escaped the wrath of the church. I happily accepted the warm wishes, comforted by the seeming security of my family's love.

CHAPTER FOUR

EARLY ADULTHOOD

WHEN THE DAY CAME TO GRADUATE FROM HIGH SCHOOL IN the spring of 2001, I had twice as much to do as my class-mates. Before it was time to walk onto the stage at the Kansas Expocentre in Topeka and accept my diploma, I'd be standing outside with my family, picketing the ceremony I would later be attending.

This did not strike me as odd or contradictory. We always picketed the local school graduations, so there was no question that we would be there. And I had to graduate from high school, so of course I would also be a participant. As I got ready on the morning of May 19, putting on my new orange organza dress from Maurice's and my white Keds, I wondered what the other students would be thinking as they filed past me and my family to go into the 10,000-seat arena—which would be half full at best, but the crowd would be made up of all my classmates and their families. My excitement about graduating began to be tempered by a prickly anxiety about how it would look to stand outside with an anti-Topeka West High School sign before heading in to join the line of soon-to-be grads.

But Gramps's voice echoed in my head, reminding me that this was an important life juncture, something the rest of us would repeat to anyone who questioned us at the picket. It was a stage in young people's lives when they'd be making important decisions about where to go and what to do next—so this was a key moment to tell them how to get on the righteous path, even if we knew none of them were actually going to take our advice.

At around ten a.m., about twenty of us gathered in front of the stadium across the large parking lot, armed with our usual Topeka West High-themed signs. In my hands was the one emblazoned with the slogan WEST FAGS—a reference to my school and their Gay Student Alliance, the GSA.

Usually, on a picket, we'd want to be holding a sign that garnered the most attention and vitriol from people passing by. I liked when people would yell at me, because it meant I was doing my job right. By this point and for the most part, instead of feeling shock and disbelief and being scared of those who disagreed with us, I learned from my family to take joy in getting an undesirable reaction. The feeling we'd get when someone would vehemently disagree with us was like the adrenaline rush you get when your favorite sports team wins a big game. Today, though, I yearned to blend in, chameleonlike. I didn't want my classmates to think I was a hypocrite, but there wasn't any way for me to get out of the picket without being yelled at by Shirl.

My friend Elizabeth and her parents passed by the picket on their way in. She'd always been someone I liked a lot. We never really talked about WBC, although I knew she knew about my involvement in it—nobody could be in school with me and miss that fact. We just acted like it wasn't a thing. We talked about homework, about singing, about volleyball—never religion. It was a bit of a weird dynamic, but it worked (and I'm proud to say we are still great friends to this day).

I smiled nervously at Elizabeth and she grinned back in return. Her parents were equally friendly, but others hurried past as if we were about to attack them.

I stayed with the picket for about half an hour, then put my sign back in the truck, grabbed my purple cap and gown out of our car, and hurried into the Expocentre. My mom and dad and siblings stayed out for a bit longer, then filed in to find seats in the gargantuan stadium. When I walked up the stage stairs to get my diploma, they cheered as loudly as any other family. They may have opposed the school on its gay policies, but they were still proud of me—and didn't see any disconnect between the two.

I was also allowed to have a graduation party, but not because the church thought it was an acceptable reason to have a party (those were reserved mostly for the monthly birthday parties we threw). This was because a French news crew was filming footage for a segment about our pickets. The family gathered in the backyard by the pool, and one of my aunts gave me a twenty-dollar gift card to Bath and Body Works. It felt weird. By church edict, nothing we did was supposed to be about us or celebrating specific people for their accomplishments. So it was hard to accept their congratulations without feeling like I was being arrogant—or being judged for accepting them. At the same time, I was expected to play up my happiness for the occasion, because there were cameras filming. I felt slightly ridiculous putting on a show for reporters just so we could get publicity, despite the fact that we had always been told we didn't have celebrations like this. It seemed hypocritical. I thought about it for a few minutes and then put it out of my head, putting a big smile on my face.

IMMEDIATELY AFTER HIGH SCHOOL, I STARTED A TWO-YEAR program at Washburn University to become a physical therapy assistant. Sara enrolled in the same program, which I was excited about; we'd always been friendly competitors academically. (There was a single instance where she scored higher than I did on a test, beating me by one point, and she celebrated all day. I was happy she got to beat me—once.) As soon as I started the program, I knew I'd want to go on and get my doctorate. I liked studying and I liked challenging myself to see how well I could do, how far I could go. I graduated from Washburn at age twenty with an associate's degree in physical therapy assistant and again at age twenty-two with my bachelor's of health science with emphasis in health administration.

I picketed both graduations, making sure I held FAG BODS, a play on the school's mascot, the Ichabod.

Going to graduate school was a tougher sell to my family. We were encouraged to get a bachelor's degree, because the family prided itself on being well educated and articulate, able to debate issues with anyone who might throw an argument our way. But when someone wanted to get a higher degree, some of the church members suspected they harbored interests other than the church's.

Nearing the end of my bachelor's degree, I applied to just one school—the only one within driving distance from my home, the University of Kansas Medical Center. To my delight and surprise, I was accepted; it's a tough school to get into. Shortly after my acceptance letter came, Megan's oldest brother Sam approached me while we were picketing the

Topeka Jewish synagogue and asked if I really needed to get my doctorate. Why, he asked, was I doing it? I knew I couldn't say I wanted to do it for myself. Everything—our occupation, our talent, our time, our energy, everything—had to be done for the good of the church, to keep the church alive and going. We were supposed to use whatever we did for a living to "help the saints"—i.e., the elders in the church. My talent was manual therapy and prescribing an exercise program for church members—massage, joint mobilizations, stretching, and making more money, so more would be tithed to the church and so I could pay for myself to go on out-of-town picket trips. I could make significantly more money if I got my doctorate, so that's what I told him. That was good enough for Sam.

He also told me that my brother had gotten his master's degree in computer science only to meet a wife. That ticked me off. How would Sam know my brother's intention in wanting to get a higher degree? Maybe Ben was like me. I had absolutely no desire to go to school to meet a spouse (indeed, I knew I was never allowed to get married, so what was the point of thinking about it?). I was going because I liked school, and wanted the highest degree possible in my profession.

DURING MY TIME IN UNDERGRAD AND AT KUMED, I PLAYED ON recreational volleyball teams once a week, reasoning that Gramps's focus on physical fitness would surely mean that my playing a sport would be acceptable to Shirl, who tended to frown on any extracurricular activities that would take us away from the church.

In undergrad, while Megan and I were playing at the university's rec center one day, a male student asked if he could join us. He said his name was Blake, and he was studying diagnostic medical sonography. I knew almost immediately that he was gay; I could just tell. He was also nice and funny and smart, and able to keep up with us on the court. We hit it off, and I hoped we'd be friends. Later, he told me, other people in the workout facility asked him if he knew who we were and why he was playing with us. He told them he didn't care, because he thought we were nice. He and I started a long-lasting friendship that day—though we wouldn't actually talk about his being gay until after I'd left the church.

SHIRL EVENTUALLY MADE ME DROP VOLLEYBALL WHILE AT KUMed because, as she said, I was "doing things I shouldn't." I wondered if she knew about my friendship with Blake and thought I was making similar ones in graduate school. I mostly got the feeling she thought I was carrying on torrid affairs or going out partying. Nothing could have been further from the truth. Even as a young adult, I behaved as I had my entire life. I wanted to be a good girl and make my parents proud of me, but this was not—and had never been—enough to make Shirl like me. So I had to quit and let my teammates down. It ruined a couple of friendships, because I was seen as unreliable. It's hard to explain to normal people in their twenties that you're still not allowed to make your own decisions about your life.

IN SEPTEMBER OF 2001, I WAS IN MY CAR ON THE WAY TO Gran and Gramps's place when a deejay broke into the song on the radio to announce that there had been an attack in New York and that two planes had been flown into the World Trade Centers. I felt a profound sense of shock and dread. As I pulled into the driveway at Gramps's place, I braced myself for what I was about to walk into.

Sure enough, family members were already gathered there, chatting about the news from New York. The tone was upbeat—elated, even. I quickly changed my facial expression to match what was going on in the room. Shirl and my uncle Jon were in the living room, literally dancing around together. "I'm so happy, it makes me want to dance a little jig!" Jon chortled.

"Awesome!" Megan exclaimed when I clustered with her and the other cousins in the hallway, discussing the news. "Yeah," I said, laughing along with her, though I couldn't help thinking it felt disrespectful to be so jubilant about so many people getting killed. I knew none of them were "innocent" in our book, but the images on the TV screens were scary and sad and I felt like I was pretending to be happy about it when I wasn't.

All day long it was an outright party, with Shirl leading the family in celebrating a particularly large-scale demonstration of God's wrath. I knew I was expected to feel the same way, and so, eventually, I did. People ask me how it's possible to be joyful about such a horrific event, but it's so easy when you've lived your whole life this way. You trust your parents and the people around you to give you the right ideas, so it becomes easy to change your mindset to match theirs. There was always some kind of logical explanation they'd have for our stance: "God did this because he's destroying the nation for disobeying him." We didn't worry about our own safety, because God was protecting us. As far as Westboro was concerned, 9/11 was our biggest I-told-you-so moment yet—and Gramps intended to use it to its full potential.

The following spring, we organized a picket of the New York firefighters. Fire department chaplain Mychal Judge, who had been the first casualty announced in the twin towers attack,

had been gay. Among our signs for the occasion was FDNY
SIN, complete with Gramps's stick-figure drawing we'd come
to refer to as the "butt buddies"—one bent over and the other
standing behind. THANK GOD FOR SEPTEMBER 11, was another,
as well as UNITED YOU'LL FALL. Mayor Giuliani was at the
center of another, with FAG ENABLER surrounding his image. It
was tough to choose between them—which would make New
Yorkers the angriest? That was what we wanted to go for.

It wasn't hard to make them angry when it came to 9/11.
Mostly, though, they reacted with sadness and shock, which
surprised me—I had been expecting (and kind of hoping for)
outright fury, which is easier to handle than tears. "How can
you say these things about men who gave their lives to protect
people?" someone asked as we picketed outside a Tribeca fire
station that had lost many of its firefighters in the collapse.
"They're not heroes," Shirl would snap. "They were just doing
their jobs. They were working to protect a fag nation that supports sin." And so it would go. We spent an hour or so in front
of the station, then moved up into midtown to protest HBO,
which was airing *The L Word*. I spotted Marc Summers, the
host of one of my favorite childhood shows, *Double Dare*, and
snapped a picture of him. He quickly walked away from me.

THE CHURCH'S FIXATION ON ARMAGEDDON INTENSIFIED AFTER
the 9/11 attacks. Along with the extra prayers and chaotic
picketing demonstrations, another extreme view was growing
in popularity among the church—that the end times prophe-
sied in the Book of Revelation were near. The church elders
were elated to witness what they believed to be the work of a
wrathful God doing divine justice unto a sinful world. Every
school shooting, mass murder, or natural disaster, here or

abroad, was also cause for celebration. Though this behavior seemed unnaturally cruel to me at first, I was still impressionable enough to be swept up in the excitement.

As the pickets progressed and became more extreme, so did the fundamentals of the church itself. For me, the most disconcerting change was in the way we prayed. Growing up, we did it solely in church services. The only people allowed to lead the prayers were the men, and Gramps or another man in the church would start with, "Let us pray." We would all bow our heads and whomever was called upon to pray would give a prayer. This seemed fairly normal to me.

Gradually everyone began praying outside of church services, too. And when we were in church, instead of merely bowing our heads, we had to sprawl out on the floor—like child's pose in yoga, or the Muslim prayer position (a religion abhorred by WBC, but mostly for the mere fact that Muslims are not WBC members, like everyone else). Even more disturbing was how the content of the prayers evolved. We actually started praying for people to die. This chilling development further chipped away at my faith and made me physically uncomfortable. I would sit quietly, hoping my face wouldn't turn red or that my breathing would become quick and noticeable. When Gramps said things that didn't sit well with me, I would try to slow down my breathing and relax my body by depressing my shoulders so it wasn't obvious to anyone that I was having a negative or anxious reaction to what he was talking about.

In 2006 came an epic lawsuit against the WBC, filed by Albert Snyder, the father of a US Marine killed in Iraq in March 2006. Snyder was accusing WBC of defamation, invasion of privacy, and intentional infliction of emotional distress after the church picketed his son's funeral in Maryland. The case eventually reached the Supreme Court in 2010, with Snyder arguing, "There is a civilized way to express an opinion in America, but it does not involve intentionally inflicting emotional distress on others."

Naturally, all church members were expected to rally around the cause. And this time we were rallying with a death wish. Though I could never bring myself to do it, most members literally began praying for Snyder to die. Although the church knew they had acted within the bounds of all local laws, church leaders reasoned that if Snyder died, the case would cease to exist. It bothered me that the church believed it held such power over another person's life or death.

"How do you pray for your enemy? Let's look at the scripture again," preached Gramps in one sermon. "We pray that we should 'be delivered from unreasonable and wicked men: for all men have not faith.' 2 Thessalonians 3:2. We pray that God's will should be done to our enemies. We pray that they should be 'anathema maranatha' (i.e., damned in hell for all eternity, and that Jesus speedily throw them into hell). 1 Corinthians 16:22. We thank God, just as Jesus did, for blinding their eyes. Matthew 11:25. We do not pray for them to be saved, just as Jesus did in John 17. Verse 9: 'I pray for them: I pray not for the world, but for them, which thou hast given me; for they are thine.' We thank God for the persecutions that we receive at their hands for His sake, because that is evidence that we have been blessed of God. Matthew 5:11."

Praying for people to die would be combined with our new all-out prayer position, spread out kneeling on the floor with our heads down. Meanwhile, when we were on an out-of-town picket and there wasn't room to pray properly, we passed a walkie-talkie so each member of the church would have a chance for their prayer to be heard.

My first attempt at praying out loud happened when I was twenty-three, on the way to a picket in Arkansas. There were six of us riding in Shirl's spotless minivan. Ben sat in the passenger seat next to Shirl. I sat in the pilot seat immediately behind her, next to Megan. A couple of Shirl's younger kids sat in the row behind us, snacking and doodling. Megan and I were talking about volleyball and discussing plans to try to beat our record of 107 volleyball bumps in a row at the next rest stop when Shirl made a sudden announcement.

"Put your snacks and your Bibles down, kids. It's prayer time!" She held up the small black device for all to see.

I immediately felt sick to my stomach.

Without further hesitation, Shirl smoothed back her long, salt-and-pepper hair and began, speaking with theatrical enthusiasm as if to demonstrate the strength of her faith and set an example for the next generation.

"Blessed Heavenly Father, we thank Thee for calling us to love and obey Thy laws and for calling us out from among this corrupt, perverted, and sinful generation. We thank Thee for each other, to exhort one another while it is called today. We thank Thee for keeping us strong and for giving us bright and shining minds so we know what we ought to do and how to present ourselves daily as we go into these mean streets. We thank Thee for opening our eyes and ears so we can see and hear what is going on around us and we thank Thee for blinding the heathen around us. We thank Thee for Thy daily displays of wrath and pray for more. We pray that Thou wilt not forget the iniquities done against this small church."

As Shirl spoke, I got more and more apprehensive, knowing it would soon be my turn to speak. My palms began to sweat and I suddenly felt the stuffy heat of the van. My feelings of claustrophobia and anxiety amplified as Shirl handed the walkie-talkie to my brother—I was next.

Ben cleared his throat before picking up where Shirl left off. "We pray that Thou will heal those who are sick among us and give us the strength, wisdom, and knowledge to get through these final days. We pray for our vile bodies to be changed into new bodies. We pray for Thy quick return when we shall meet Thee in the sky with our new bodies and rule and reign with Thee forever."

It was my turn. I took the walkie-talkie from Ben and fumbled it for a moment, trying to remember which button to press. I found the talk button, pushed it, and started my prayer with a weak voice.

"We pray that Thou will be with us as we go out into the battlefield." I stopped suddenly, choking on the word "battlefield." My face flushed with embarrassment as I lifted my finger off the talk button. The absurdity of the situation—being trapped in this van and forced to pray for the downfall of humanity into this little walkie-talkie—hit me all at once. I looked over to Megan, desperate to tell her how I felt. But although she was my best friend, she was also Shirl's daughter, and always played the part of faithful, obedient servant. She smiled at me encouragingly.

"I get nervous!" I said apologetically. Ben turned back to look at me and began to laugh. I knew what they wanted me to say. They wanted me to pray for evil to befall all of mankind and for God's love and grace to be with us and His hatred and anger to be poured down onto the rest of the world. But as fearful as I was of Shirl's temper, and as much as I wanted to please my family in order to just get it over with, I couldn't bring myself to do it. I didn't feel it and I couldn't say it.

Noticing Shirl's furious expression, Ben stopped laughing. My eyes swelled with tears as I passed the walkie-talkie to Megan.

"We pray for . . ." she dutifully continued the prayer.

I sat quietly, my head reeling from the humiliation of what had just happened, and it wasn't until we made our next stop in southwest Missouri twenty minutes later that I was able to really cry and catch my breath.

While Shirl and the others were in the bathroom, Megan found me sobbing in the parking lot. She gently put her hand on my shoulder as she had so many times growing up. "Praying out loud is new to everyone. You'll get used to it." She gave me her sweet, toothy smile. A gust of cold wind blew in from the highway, tossing a strand of brown hair loose from her braided ponytail. With her light blue eyes and long curly hair, she could, at times, look just like her mother—only not terrifying.

I shoved my hands in the front pouch of my pink hoodie, still shivering, though the breeze had passed. I looked down at Megan's long, bare legs. Also like her mother, Megan chose to wear shorts when most people would find them inappropriate or, at the very least, unseasonable. "I just don't know what to say," I told her, which was only half true.

"All you need to do is listen to what others are saying and you'll get it," she said. "Don't worry too much about it."

I knew Megan didn't understand the real problem I had with the prayers, but she so devoutly followed the practices of the church that I couldn't bring myself to tell her the truth. Even so, talking to Megan made me feel better. We hugged and joked about trying for the bump record at the next stop.

But I never got used to the new prayers. There was something wrong with me, something different—I couldn't find it in my heart to pray for these horrible things to happen. Despite my constant inner turmoil, I did eventually manage to force myself through a public prayer. But I chose my words very carefully, walking the narrow line between what was expected of me and what I was willing to say. Still my blood pressure rose, my heart raced, and I broke out in a nervous sweat during every prayer I gave from then on.

THOSE INTENSIFIED PRAYERS BOTHERED ME MORE THAN ANY of the actual pickets. I had been picketing since I was eight years old, and it had become second nature to me. Marching up and down a busy street with a GOD HATES FAGS sign and telling everyone God hated them and they were going to hell was just another Saturday afternoon for me, and I never questioned or took the time to contemplate the nature of what I was doing. As I got older, it got easier and easier to disconnect and simply go through the motions. Even though I'd been in the middle of some extremely intense picket situations, none of them were as heart-rending as having to personally deliver a prayer full of hate.

It was around this time that church members started saying Gramps was losing faith. Church members were told to not talk to Gramps. It was the beginning of his ouster from his own congregation.

The family made sure to hide this internal conflict from a visitor who'd shown up to do a TV documentary on the church: British reporter Louis Theroux, who shot for three weeks for a documentary called *The Most Hated Family in America*. He had a well-deserved reputation for getting under people's skin through his cheerful, faux-naive demeanor. But he met his match in my family, where we had spent our entire lives being relentlessly friendly to everyone—especially people who were trying to discredit the church. In an article about the time he spent with us, Louis wrote, "I found a lot to like about the Phelps[es]. They have a strong family unit, and Gramps aside, they were open and hospitable. It was fascinating to see the power of a family to create its own bizarre ideology and pass it down through the generations. But I guess I'll be seeing you all in hell." Cheeky though he was, Louis had more of an impact on me than I realized in the moment; he repeatedly asked me if I didn't yearn to get out in the world and make decisions for myself, and those questions rolled around in my head long after he and the film crew were gone.

WE MADE OUR FIRST VIDEO PARODY AROUND THE SAME TIME. It was of Jay Z's "Big Pimpin'," with Megan writing the words to a parody called "Big Fibbin'." She studied up on Jay Z and rap in general. This would not be just a chant for pickets but an actual video. The videographer would be Steve Drain, the new arrival to the church.

I'd never liked Steve or his teenage daughter Lauren very much, simply based on their rude, egomaniacal personalities. Steve had showed up at the church initially aiming to shoot a documentary on Gramps and the church called *Hatemongers*, a movie that would be critical of the supposed cultlike atmosphere of WBC. But after a series of long conversations with Gramps, Steve did a complete about-face—the first and, I believe, only time Gramps had ever successfully converted someone—and moved his family to Topeka to join Westboro. It was never really a natural fit. Steve Drain was bossy and condescending, and I didn't think he and his family had any place within mine. But it was a victory for Gramps to have actually convinced a sinner to see the light and join the only true religion. And we couldn't deny that Steve's skills would be useful in an age when video was becoming the predominant way of getting our message out.

We set to film one warm, late-summer day in 2007. Before we went anywhere, Steve stopped us with a little speech. "Now I don't mind doing this," he said, "but all of you need to step up and start doing more. I know this is fun, but not everything is fun and games. All of you need to help out more. If you see something that needs to be done, you fill the gap. You know, if you see someone needs help with their kids or help with housework, you do it, you fill that gap. OK?"

We all looked at each other, wide-eyed. This guy was reprimanding us? He'd been around for a relatively short time. He didn't know what we did or didn't do to help out. And the implication that we were a bunch of slackers—which couldn't have been further from the truth—was obnoxious. It was like he was yelling at us for something he'd just made up. But we all nodded dutifully: "OK." Looking pleased with himself, he walked off to the set we'd put together in Shirl's basement. The exchange made me highly uncomfortable, but I quickly got excited again about the project, because I was with my friends. It turned out to be a fun day. We had gone out and bought costume jewelry for the shoot: giant $ necklaces and big, fake-diamond GANGSTA rings. I worried someone would be mad that I wasn't wearing an official church T-shirt, but I figured a brown tank top looked better for the song. Jael wore her orange SIGN-MOVIES.NET hoodie, despite the oppressive heat that day. We shot against a backdrop of picket signs in the basement, then moved on to the backyard and to our favorite picket spot at 17th and Gage for our walking-down-the-street shots. Steve turned very professional once we started shooting, and all the girls got along well despite the presence of Steve's daughter,

'm picketing with my cousin, Megan, in Greensboro, North Carolina, at the
Southern Baptist Convention. We were always told to look happy and joyous
when proclaiming God's word to the masses. June 2006.

Picketing a soldier's funeral in Maryland, May 2006. The police set up a bar-
icade of orange cones for us to stand behind. Patriot Guard motorcycles are
parked across the street.

Our finished product from our shirt party. Top row left to right: Shirl, Megan, Libby, Jael, Katherine. Bottom row left to right: Bekah, Sara, Lauren. June 2006.

'm picketing with my nephew, Seth, at an out-of-town picket in Los Angeles.
Lucy Drain is in the background. October 2007.

Before the picketing began, my cousins and I frequently got together to play. I'm with my cousins, Jael and Megan, playing in a sandbox. 1989.

The church men are playing a game of basketball in the backyard of the church. Summer 2008.

I'm holding my go-to TURN OR BURN sign at one of the earlier pickets. This was well before the sign shop times and all signs were handmade. My sister, Sara, is holding GOD HATES FAGS and our church friend, Katherine Hockenbarger, is holding FAG = AIDS. 1995.

The picture of me with my sister, Sara, in bikinis. This is the picture that WBC members questioned me about, which ultimately led to the intervention and my departure.

Me with my sister, Sara, plus Gran and Gramps at my twenty-fourth and my sister's twenty-sixth birthday party. April 2007.

Logan and I in front of the Eiffel Tower in Paris, France, during a vacation we took together in summer 2010. No one is allowed to leave the country while at WBC. This was my first trip outside of the country. We went to England, Belgium, the Netherlands, Germany, Austria, Italy, Switzerland, and France.

Logan and I swimming in a cenote in Mexico on our honeymoon. July 2011

Logan and I with our children: Paxton, two, and Zea, nine months. We're teaching our children to be kind and accepting of everyone. September 2016.

Logan and I on our wedding day in Cozumel, Mexico. July 9, 2011.

NoH8 photo shoot with the amazing Adam Bouska and his lovely boyfriend, Jeff Parshley, at the Equality House. April 2014. Left to right: my friend Blake, me, Paxton, Logan, Davis, and Amelia Markham, who works at the Equality House.

I'm writing a positive message in response to vandalism on the Equality House. January 2017.

who had the reputation of making up stories about us to make trouble. I stayed away from her as much as possible during the shoot and everything went smoothly. We all had fun laughing and making up dance moves, and the tension with Steve Drain was momentarily forgotten.

In 2008 came another shift for the church—a focus on the White House. After Barack Obama's historic election, the church closely studied scripture and concluded that the president was in fact the Beast himself—the Antichrist manifested as a symbol of the end of days. It was written in Revelation commentary that the people of the world would not see the Antichrist as a fire-breathing beast, but rather as a beautiful, brilliant, and charismatic friend to the world. To the church, the new president met all of those qualifications. They saw Obama as one-third of the hellish trinity that mocks the Holy Trinity: the Dragon (Satan), the Beast (Obama), and the False Prophet (the Pope).

Gramps introduced this idea in a fiery sermon, as he had done with many other bombastic theories, and the idea spread like wildfire throughout our little community. Citing Revelation 13, he preached that Obama had "risen out of the sea of troubled humanity" to "capture the imagination of the world." My grandfather accused Obama of "blasphemy against the Holy Ghost," because he valued some parts of the Bible while choosing to ignore others. He also said that Obama was guilty of using the "bully pulpit" of presidency to lead this nation and the world to believe blasphemous things against God.

Partially, we targeted Obama because he was the biggest political figure, thereby guaranteeing we'd get press if we picketed him. But Obama made a particularly good target for us. He was relatively young for a presidential candidate, and was seen as *so* cool. Many kids my age were really excited about him. It was obvious to Gramps and the others that he supported the homosexual agenda, even before he came out and said that he was in favor of gay marriage. We started calling him Antichrist Obama pretty early on.

When the picket request went out for people to go to Washington, DC, for his inauguration, I signed up eagerly and Shirl gave her consent. I knew it was going to be a big event, and I wanted to be a part of it. Lots of us did, but only twelve of us were picked to go—I was a little surprised that I'd passed muster with Shirl for such a major event, and I wondered if Megan had leaned on her a little to let me go. Marge, Steve, Megan, Bekah, Katherine, Grace, Isaiah, Abi, Jael, Tim, and I, plus Shirl, made up the group that left for Dulles Airport on the night of January 19, 2009.

When we boarded the shuttle in Washington to get our rental cars, I sat next to an older black man and noticed a giant ring on his finger. "Did you play basketball?" I asked him. He told me that he had once been the physical therapist for a black basketball league before they joined the NBA. "That's so awesome!" I said. I told him I'd just graduated from physical therapy school, and we talked shop until we reached the rental car building.

It was blustery and very cold the next morning when we had to get up at the Days Inn before dawn to be at our police-appointed spot near a barricade. I pulled on layer after layer: gray ski pants, giant black mittens, a few layered jackets with a fur-hooded purple vest over them, and a ski hat to keep my ears from freezing.

As we waited in line to go through the metal detectors for the inauguration route, the man from the shuttle was right next to me—out of thousands of people, he was the one I'd ended up next to. I gave him a smile. I was a little embarrassed; I didn't think he knew I was with the church since we didn't have our signs out yet. I was nervous, though. It wasn't like I had built a strong friendship with this man, but something about the situation definitely made me feel awkward—I couldn't quite put my finger on it. I was supposed to always be proud of who and what I was.

Even before the sun came up, there were people starting to appear along the streets. A lot of them were black, I noticed. The cops near us were wearing riot gear helmets, the kind with the visors that can be pulled down. We got into place and held up our signs; I had picked an Obama one that had a picture of him with horns on his head. We wanted to get the biggest reaction we could out of people. We wanted all of their hate.

Another sign bore the words THE BEAST and pictured a frog coming out of Obama's mouth. That was from Revelation 16: "And I saw three unclean spirits like frogs come out of the mouth of the dragon, out of the mouth of the beast, out of the mouth of the false prophet." There was a sign about abortion, because the new president believed in abortion; it had a picture of a bloody baby on it.

Some people talked to us as they walked by; most just looked shocked or dismissive. "You guys are so stupid," one said. "This is ridiculous," another laughed. "You guys voted for a fag enabler!" we shouted back. There were cops every four or five feet nearby. Everywhere around us people were wearing Obama shirts and hats and pins; if you didn't have one, you could buy them from the many vendors on street corners.

None of these people knew what we did: that Obama was going to be the last president and that the Lord was going to come back during his tenure. As for me, I felt relatively indifferent. I believed what I was told, so it was easy for me to parrot the teachings of my grandfather. Later on, I would notice certain things that I liked about Obama—that he would do the Final Four picks, or read to kids on the White House lawn.

In the moment, though, I mostly just thought it was amazing that I got to go to a presidential inauguration, even if I was picketing it. Vice President Biden drove by us in a limo at one point, shaking his head in dismay. We never did see the president himself.

After a couple of hours, we left for the airport. Everyone felt good about the presence we'd had there, talking about how Biden had come by. "We were the biggest story of that inauguration," Shirl assured us while we waited for our plane. "They will all be talking about us and our signs." She was sure to speak loud enough so everyone waiting could hear her. We'd stolen Obama's thunder, we were sure.

Obama would become a frequent sermon topic during the years that followed. We got a lot of online feedback about our campaign against him: "Why do you hate Obama?" people would ask. "We don't hate him," we would write back. "God hates him. We're just the messenger. We're the people that love you."

As a young adult, I was still grappling with the topic of sexuality. Sex remained a terrifying and taboo subject. In one physical therapy class, a teacher asked us if any of our patients had complained about not being able to have sex, or of pain while having sex. I raised my hand and began to describe one man who'd told me back pain was keeping him from being able to do it . . . I couldn't say the word "sex." (I still have trouble saying it today.)

"What did you tell him?" the teacher asked me. "I told him, 'I'm not going to talk about this,'" I admitted. I told her

I thought it was inappropriate talk. My teacher treated me kindly for that, suggesting other ways I could have approached it. There were a few instructors who didn't take so kindly to my presence in their classes, though. There were some clinics that didn't want to work with me because of my last name; they'd call my school and say they didn't want me there because of my affiliation with the church.

BUT A CHANCE ENCOUNTER AT THE LAW LIBRARY AT WASHBURN, where I worked when I was wasn't studying, helped nudge me toward a little more awareness of sexual attraction. One of my jobs there was pushing carts of law books around, putting them away. It was harder than you'd think. Puzzlingly, they didn't use the Dewey Decimal System to know where some of the books would go, so I had to ask for help a lot. It was kind of humiliating, but I always liked meeting the people who were studying there.

One day while I was pushing the cart around on the second floor, I saw a guy sitting at one of the big rectangular communal tables. He was surrounded by stacks of books, and he was really cute: tall and muscular. I liked his skin color. I thought he must be half black. I liked his looks; I had never really thought white guys were all that cute, though I'd always been mostly surrounded by them in Kansas.

The thought of approaching him made me nervous. But this was my job, I told myself, putting the books away. Just my job, nothing else. I asked him if he was done with any of the big law books that surrounded him at the table. I was hoping he would tell me he was still using them, so I wouldn't have to look like an idiot trying to figure out where they went, but he said he was done with them. He was really nice. Gentle. When

I sheepishly asked him where they'd come from, he didn't act like I was an idiot.

He asked me what my name was, and where I was from. He said his name was Enrique, and he was a Washburn graduate student, studying family law. He was trying to have a conversation with me, and I didn't know how to handle it at all. It made me realize that I didn't know how to have a real conversation with anyone, really, if it wasn't about picketing. We're not supposed to talk about ourselves in the church. Nothing is supposed to be about us, only about praising God. So I always felt bad talking about myself. Getting increasingly uncomfortable, I wanted to get away from him and get back to the book cart. I knew talking to him would have been considered "messing around" by my family. When we have a job outside the church, we're supposed to go there, do our work, and come home. No messing around. Definitely no conversations with handsome strange men.

After that, though, he would come in a lot. In spite of myself, I began to think it was because I was working there. He just seemed to stand up a little straighter when he walked by me, and sometimes I could tell he was looking at me out of the corner of his eye. One time he came in and asked me where the Bible was, and I thought that was probably to impress me. He'd found out about my family connection somehow—he never would tell me how. But it didn't seem to put him off talking to me. He even told me he had worked with my uncle, Tim, at the local jail years ago.

Gradually, I got more comfortable talking to him. One day, he came in to check a book out, and looked me over as I was checking it out for him. I was wearing a black shirt that day, with an oval neckline that hung off the shoulder a bit.

"Your shirt is funny-looking," he said with a mischievous smile.

"Well, your face is funny-looking!" I shot back, then froze. We said that kind of stuff to each other all the time at the church, but not to anyone else. *Oh my gosh*, I thought, *he's going to stop talking to me now*. He started to laugh, though. He seemed to like the way I talked to him. I didn't know how to flirt like other girls my age did.

One of his favorite subjects was black rights and reparations. He was convinced that he should get money and reparations from the slave era, and we would argue about that frequently.

"You are not a slave!" I told him. "If you were a slave, you should get something. But you're not. And you get scholarships for being a minority. I don't get that." He would just start laughing at me. He would say stuff to me to get me riled up. I said, "I'm getting sick of arguing with you about this." But I wasn't, not really.

Eventually, I started physical therapy school and left my job at the library. I thought that would be the end of my friendship with him. But one day during our regular daily picket, at the corner of 17th Street and Gage, Enrique showed up. I was holding my usual TURN OR BURN sign. He parked his car by the side of the road and strolled over to me. I didn't know what to do. I didn't want to get in trouble for talking to him. But he came over, grinning at me, and told me he was campaigning for a local politician named Hurd. He gave me a pamphlet, and said that we should all vote for this guy. My cousins and aunts and uncles looked at me suspiciously; why was this guy so friendly with me? Feeling desperate to convince my family I wasn't messing around, I started a chant of

"Hurd the Turd." Enrique just smiled, unfazed, and walked away. Immediately my relatives started questioning me: "Who was that? What was he doing?" I shrugged it off, but I couldn't help blushing.

AT CHURCH ONE MORNING, I APPROACHED TIM AND SAID, "I met someone who used to work with you." I told him it was Enrique. I was taken aback at how mad and protective and defensive my uncle immediately got. "Why are you talking to that guy? I'm gonna do something about this." I didn't understand why he'd reacted like that. I had zero intentions of having a boyfriend; it wasn't on my radar. It wasn't a possibility. I had been told none of the rest of us were ever going to be in relationships or get married, and I wasn't rebelling against that. I was worried he would make a big deal out of it. Why had I said anything in the first place?

Months later, right after graduating from physical therapy school, we were picketing at the law school when Enrique pulled up at the picket and waved for me to come over. I was really happy to see him, though I didn't want to show it in front of my family.

"Hey, I haven't seen you in a long time," he said with a smile. The way he said it, I knew he had missed me. He told me about his work in child placement and divorce cases. We exchanged emails, and started writing a little bit. He mentioned that his back was hurting, and I told him, "I can work on that, if you want to stop by sometime."

The next week, he came to the office where I was working as a physical therapist. I tried to be as businesslike as possible, but I was beyond excited to see him. I brought him into the tiny treatment room, had him sit on the treatment table, and

GIRL ON A WIRE

turned my back to get lotion. When I turned around, he was standing right there behind me—and he kissed me. I was really shocked. It was my first kiss. I was twenty-five. I recovered my wits a second later and recoiled a bit, but he swooped in and kissed me again. This time I kissed him back.

"Slow down," he said with a laugh. I confessed that it was my first time, which didn't seem to surprise him. "I'll show you how to do it," he said with a smile. Worried someone would catch us, I told him to take off his shirt and lie down on his stomach. I tried not to look at him as an attractive man but as a patient, nothing more. I worked on his back like I'd said I would. Afterward, we went out to his car, where he kissed me again before he left. It made my knees weak. I couldn't believe what I had just done.

Over the next few months, I saw him several more times. Quite a few meetings into our tryst, he told me he had a girlfriend. I knew nothing was going to happen with him in the long run, because he would cheat on me just like he was cheating on his current girlfriend. I knew it was wrong to see him. But I couldn't resist when he called. The kissing, and everything else, was so much fun—I couldn't believe I'd never done it before. It was so good that I forgot to worry that I was going to hell for doing it, at least until I was driving home afterward. But I still didn't want to disappoint my family, my parents, and I knew that disappointment was inevitable from Marge who had had sex with somebody and gotten pregnant. I knew it was wrong. So I tried to keep busy with whatever they wanted me to do. I was worried about my parents finding out and kicking me out of the church.

A FEW SHORT MONTHS AFTER I GRADUATED WITH MY doctorate in physical therapy and got a full-time job, Shirl immediately asked me to take Mondays off. I'm sure she knew this was going to be a tough thing for a new hire to ask her boss, but she demanded it of me anyway. She told me I needed to help out more with watching children, going to the noon pickets, filing at the law office, doing yard work, and running errands for the church. It felt to me as though she wanted me to get fired or give the job up voluntarily, that she was trying to keep me from straying too far or seeing too much of the outside world. She never seemed to feel I'd done enough.

Soon, I was babysitting for eight hours at a stretch on my days off. Resentment began to build up in me. I loved being around kids and helping out, but if I'd wanted to watch children all day, I'd have taken courses in child development. I certainly wouldn't have a chance to have my own children, as my aunts had long ago decreed that no one else in the church was going to be getting married going forward. I finally broke down and vented to my mother about it, worrying all the while that she'd take the complaint back to headquarters—in other words, Shirl. I'd be in trouble for two things: not having a positive attitude about helping the church, and not being totally honest about all my feelings all the time. The fact that these two things were often in opposition to each other didn't enter into it for Shirl. My mom agreed with me, that Shirl was requiring too much of me and her demands were outrageous. She understood where I was coming from, but she too was fearful of Shirl's lashing out if someone dared question her authority.

ANOTHER THING SHIRL DEMANDED OF ME WAS TO REGULARLY lead a picket with my younger cousins. One of them took a menacing turn.

It was our duty to get five to ten church members to our regular daily picket site at 17th and Gage. One sunny summer afternoon in 2003, Josh and I assembled a group to walk up to the site: Josh's younger siblings Megan and Gabe, and Jael with her younger brothers Jacob and Josh (whom we referred to jokingly as Little Josh, because he was bigger than the older Josh). We carpooled in my white Toyota Corolla, while Josh took Gabe in his family's red Chevy pickup. His truck held some signs and two of our upside-down flags—one American and one Kansan.

We parked on my street, Holly Lane, and walked to the side of the park across the street from the two churches we regularly picketed. As we set up on the corner, the girls holding the littlest signs and the two Joshes holding the biggest ones, a man came out of the trees behind us. As he walked toward us, I could see he had a weathered face, shaggy, graying hair, and dirty face and clothes.

"Y'all out here picketing," he snarled. "Flags upside down. Y'all are fucking pieces of shit." He came to the girls' side first, and we ignored him, as we had been trained to do time and again. It wasn't easy, though, pretending the grown man screaming in our faces didn't exist. Finally, he moved along toward Josh, who told little Gabe to get behind him. He grabbed Josh's sign and a tug-of-war ensued, which Josh won—as everyone does to win tug-of-war—by letting up a little, then yanking the sign out of the man's hands completely.

The man staggered almost completely into the street. Josh got out his phone and dialed 911, as we always did if we were being physically threatened in any way. The girls, in the meantime, went into fight mode: Jael and I had disassembled the flags and were wielding the rods from them like bats. Megan held her sign aloft, ready to swing it if necessary. Finally the man left—but it took a lot longer for all of us to relax. It was getting scarier all the time to be out on the street with our message. We were always peaceful—why weren't our opponents? Why was everyone getting so mad at our signs? We were doing the most loving thing anyone could do for a person: telling them that if they didn't repent, they'd end up in a terrible place, where fire shoots out of their eyeballs. But I also had to admit that just as I was finding our message to be more and more extreme, maybe others were seeing it too, and having more and more extreme reactions.

It wasn't long afterward that Josh made the decision to leave the church.

IT WAS AROUND THIS TIME THAT I BECAME MORE AWARE OF THE sexual comments from people passing by. A gay man saying he would turn straight if he could get a piece of me, and people pulling over because they thought I was "fucking hot" were two of the most minor words and gestures thrown my way. Some of them were so obscene they left me speechless, or in tears.

I regularly stood by the big fountain next to the Washburn University sign at the corner and turned my big GOD HATES AMERICA sign toward traffic. Some of my aunts would go to this picket to get some exercise; they would walk up one side of the sidewalk, turn around and walk back, then walk up the other sidewalk before repeating. Across the street to the north was a fraternity, and they didn't hesitate to come out regularly to show their displeasure with us by yelling "Go home." They also didn't hesitate to come out and yell at me when I would run around the school alone for exercise, only this time their yells were catcalls. I would look down and wonder what on earth had made them target me—as usual, I'd be dressed in athletic clothing, nothing revealing or suggestive.

Not long afterward, I was informed by Shirl that I had broken the 4B rule: No showing your boobs, belly, back, or butt. It was the first time I had heard that rule; I felt pretty sure she just made it up for the occasion. My V-neck shirt was deemed too scandalous, apparently—even though my intention in wearing it was most definitely not to attract the opposite sex; V-necks were more comfortable! When I brought up this point, it was brushed aside as nonsense. I was scolded most for the way I reacted to my verbal punishment, but all I did was remind them of what others had done in the past. Questioning their authority was forbidden. But enough was enough. What if one day I had more serious objections and wasn't able to express myself? This was no way to live.

CHAPTER FIVE

LEAVING

"Don't you dare start to cry. There are counter-protestors across the street and they have cameras, and they're not gonna see you cry," said Shirl, clenching her teeth through a forced smile.

Traffic at the intersection of 17th and Gage was at a constant flow on this sunny Saturday afternoon in 2009, and cars honked at regular intervals in response to a small Honk for Love sign held by a counter-protestor on the other side of the street. The cheap cardboard sign contrasted sharply with the six-foot-tall, laminated God Hates You sign I was holding.

"Don't you think for one second you're gonna run to your mom because Megan and the other girls are shunning you," she continued. "If you weren't misbehaving, they'd have no reason to shun you!" Shirl stuck a bony, well-manicured finger in my face as she spoke and rose up on the balls of her feet, trying to match my height. She leaned in so close the bill of her baseball cap almost touched my nose. I could smell the bitter stench of coffee on her breath.

I wanted to turn to the small group of protestors, who looked just like me or anyone else, and let them know I was upset and why. I didn't think the way Shirl was treating people in the church, including myself, was right. But all I could do was stare down into her dark eyes, barely visible through her thick sunglasses, and bite my tongue.

"This is gonna get real messy, real fast," she said as she turned her back to me and marched down the sidewalk with her GOD IS YOUR ENEMY picket sign held high above her head. Her ponytail hung through the back opening of her hat in a long braid, reaching past the middle of her pink GODHATESFAGS. COM T-shirt.

As I caught my breath and attempted to pull myself together, I imagined, if only for a moment, a life unrestrained by Shirl's sharp tongue and disapproving glare. I was twenty-five now, but Shirl still treated me like a child and never hesitated to criticize or scold me. I was relieved her outburst had ended, but I knew it was only a matter of time before she was going to be on me again, which seemed to be happening with more and more frequency. Our latest clash, earlier that week, had brought her near the boiling point. What I didn't know was that in only a few days' time, I'd be free of her forever.

TWO MONTHS EARLIER, I HAD BEEN EXCITED WHEN MY PARENTS announced that we were going to Puerto Rico for our yearly weeklong vacation. The night before we left, I took a break from packing to see what my sister Sara was up to. I found her sitting on the floor of her bedroom in front of a stack of neatly folded clothes and an open suitcase.

"Get out! Why do you always barge in like that?" Sara shrieked.

"I knocked while I opened the door. That's good enough, right?" I smiled a big, goofy smile, jutting my head forward. I got a kick out of how much it annoyed her when I did that.

"Whatever. What do you want?" she asked impatiently, as she picked up an old pair of pink flip-flops for inspection.

"Well," I said excitedly, "I got these two bikinis from Meg at work. She gave them to me because she hasn't used them since she got pregnant three years ago. Do you want one?" I also got a kick out of giving presents. "I like this one better because of all the bright colors, but I'll let you have it because it's smaller," I said, holding up the vibrant, multicolored, floral printed bikini. "This is the one I'll wear." It was a dark brown bikini with a single pink flower design in the upper corner.

"I like mine better," she said with a grin, holding it up for closer inspection.

"I know! I love all the bright colors, but it will fit you better, so I guess you can have it. You should pack it right now so you don't forget it," I told her, happy she liked the gift.

"Thanks . . . but can you leave now so I can finish packing?"

"OK, bye," I said, and headed back to my room to do the same.

FAMILY VACATIONS WERE ALWAYS SOMETHING I LOOKED forward to. We went almost exclusively to beaches or mountains, and either lay on the beach and swam or went on hikes. We discussed the magnificence of God, and how He was responsible for the Earth's beauty.

Puerto Rico didn't disappoint. We snorkeled, surfed, and hiked through huge, magnificent forests. Growing up, I had gone on countless hikes with my family, and I always valued the sense of closeness I got from sharing an adventure with them. Like any adventure, there were usually a few bumps along the way, like when my dad would carefully follow the map to the only closed gate of entry into the park, which we could laugh and tease him about later. It was especially nice to be away from the church community for a while. It was almost unheard of to go on a trip that wasn't arranged around some picketing event, and I had one of the best times of my life.

WHEN WE GOT BACK HOME, I WAS EAGER TO TELL GRAMPS and Gran about our trip. Sara and I found Gran in the kitchen humming a hymn as she wiped the counters in her signature red sweater, her hair wrapped in a bun at the nape of her neck. The kitchen, as usual, smelled of Dawn dish soap. We told her we had come to tell them about our trip, and she got on the phone and buzzed upstairs to Gramps to tell him to come down and listen.

I was relieved he wasn't working on a sermon. Now I could sit down with my grandparents and tell them about Puerto Rico, instead of the usual talk about God's wrath and the damnation of the world.

"Hey, lovebugs. How've you been?" Gramps smiled as he shuffled slowly but surely down the stairs in his tennis shoes, athletic shorts, and a purple Minnesota Vikings football jersey. On his way through the kitchen, he stopped and grabbed a sandwich from the refrigerator. He sat down by Gran on a stool across the tall, cream-colored table from Sara and me, unwrapped a veggie Subway sub, and announced he was ready to listen.

"It was probably the best trip I've ever been on. It was just so beautiful!" I began, breathless with excitement. "We went to this awesome lighthouse on the southwest part of the island; it was breathtaking. The guide told us a lot of movies had been shot there. They were actually shooting a movie while we were there, and I got a picture of this guy doing karate moves. We almost didn't make it up to the lighthouse because the roads were so bad and bumpy, but I'm glad we kept going to see it! And there's this water we went in at night that would light up when we touched it." Sara sat by silently, smiling and nodding, as she was used to doing when I had a wave of excitement come over me.

"How does that happen? How does the water light up?" asked Gran, interested.

"There are microorganisms that sparkle for a little bit when they're agitated," I said. "It's called a bioluminescent bay and there are only a few in the world. I'll have to show you a picture of us in it."

"Did you get any pictures of you two girls together? I haven't had one of you girls in a long time," asked Gramps, taking a moment away from his sandwich.

"Sure, I can look through them and give you a good one," I said.

That evening, I looked through the photos, searching for the best one to give them. My personal favorite was a picture of Sara and me in our bikinis on the beach near the Los Morrillos Lighthouse. I ordered an eight-by-ten of the photo, put it in a silver frame, and eagerly took it to my grandparents the following week. They placed it front and center on their dining room table, where they displayed a few religious books and a small collection of family photos. The table was also used to collect tithe at the beginning of each church service, so every member of the church was sure to see it.

I didn't give much more thought to the photo until the end of the following church service, which as always took place at Gran and Gramps's house. I noticed that the picture had been pushed to the very back of the table and was now mostly blocked by the other books and photos. My heart dropped. I wondered why it had been pushed to the back. All I could think of was the bikinis. I grabbed the picture and ran out the door without saying a word to anyone.

I WENT HOME AND PREPARED TO BE REPRIMANDED BY MY family. My plan was to keep quiet and pray that everything would blow over. I rationalized that since the picture was all but invisible, it couldn't cause anyone any more grief, and they'd probably soon forget about it. On my way back from a picket the next day, I got a call from Megan.

"Libby, why were you wearing a bikini in that picture you gave to Gramps and Gran?" she asked. Here we go, I thought. My body tensed.

"A girl I work with had a couple of them before she got pregnant and had her baby. She didn't want them anymore, so she gave them to me," I said, as calmly and matter-of-factly as I could manage.

"Well, we've been talking," Megan said, "and no one thinks it's appropriate to wear that."

"*We?*" I thought to myself. I guessed she meant her and her mother. "You've worn one before!" I said out loud, incredulous.

"That was when I was twelve!" she said. Even though Megan was my best friend, she, like her mother, still expected me to immediately apologize when confronted by a displeased church member.

"OK, well you wore one before and I didn't think it was that big of a deal." I spoke quickly and hung up the phone, hands shaking. This was the first time I had ever stood up for myself against another member of the church. Megan was surely going to tell Shirl, who would in turn call everyone in the church to inform them of my disobedience. The whole issue had gotten blown way out of proportion—but this, as I was soon to learn, was just the beginning.

I saw Megan at a picket the next day. Traffic at 17th and Washburn was steady on this overcast afternoon, and the occasional car honked as they drove by, some with passengers who flipped us off as they passed. Megan and I set up with our GOD HATES YOUR TEARS and FAG BODS signs on the landscaped grassy terrace in front of the school's fountain. My aunts Rachel and Becky were down closer to the street, chatting while walking up and down the sidewalks, turning their signs to greet the oncoming traffic. They were regulars at this location; they considered it a good place to walk for some easy exercise.

I was hoping to put the whole bikini drama behind me, but Megan brought it up almost immediately. She reminded me of the 4B rule. I tried to explain that this bikini was no more revealing than any other; I considered the swimsuit to be adequately modest. Seeing that she was still displeased, I gave in and apologized, hoping it would resolve the issue once and for all.

The next day, I stopped by Gramps's house on my way home from a busy day at work. He had been complaining of pain going down his right leg and wanted me to use my physical therapy skills to try to fix his back. I had been helping him for a few weeks by this point, and we were in mid-routine when my phone rang. It was Shirl.

She told me she wanted me to go down to her house because a few people wanted to talk to me. I squeaked out an "OK," and hung up, panic-stricken. I tried to restrain my tears to avoid upsetting Gramps and Gran, but simply couldn't; I burst into tears.

"What's going on, hon?" asked Gramps, turning to me with a concerned look.

"You remember that picture you asked for—of me and Sara?" I asked, struggling to get the words out. Gramps nodded. "Well, we got in trouble for wearing bikinis."

"That's not right," he said. "I think you both look great in that picture," he added.

"But it was the way I reacted to them when they told me not to wear it, so now they want me to go over to Shirl's house and talk to people."

"We'll come with you," said Gramps.

We both knew what was in store for me: when a church member committed a wrongdoing and it was seen as severe, Shirl called a meeting for an intervention. My bikini offense, and my initial reluctance to apologize, had been deemed severe enough to qualify. I was absolutely devastated by what I knew would shortly happen. The judgment and vitriol of the whole church was about to be unleashed on me. I was to be the sole target of a massive, coordinated verbal firing squad that had but one purpose—to tear me down, put me in my place. Their aim was to make me so frightened, so humiliated, so ashamed, that I'd never find the courage to challenge them again.

I was grateful for Gramps and Gran wanting to come and show support. They offered to come, I think, in hopes that the group might be a little less hostile with them there. The problem was that Gramps and Gran never attended these meetings unless an offense was serious enough to involve them, and I was afraid that their presence might only further enrage the other members. But I couldn't bring myself to ask them not to come, and told them I'd meet them at Shirl's.

I WAS OVERCOME WITH WORRY AS I WALKED ACROSS THE BLOCK toward Shirl's house. I had never felt so disconnected from my own life. The air was cool that March evening and the crickets were beginning to chirp. I was exhausted and miserable, and my head throbbed from a sinus infection that had begun a few days prior. I had been witness to several of these interventions in the past, when other members had been accused of stepping out of line. Just attending these meetings had always filled me with anxiety; the thought of being the subject of the church's merciless scrutiny was almost unbearable. The rejuvenated feeling I had gained from my family vacation was gone completely—I just wanted to go to sleep.

As I neared the door, I thought of the movie *The Green Mile*, imagining myself as condemned to a desolate fate, taking that slow march toward my hour of persecution. The fact that the meeting had been called meant that the verdict had already been handed down. There'd be no chance to defend myself, no opportunity to plead my case, and no one to turn to for support. I was painfully aware of the possibility they had already decided to kick me out, and I took a last look behind me before entering the side door of the house, fearing it might be the last time I made this walk—a walk I'd made a thousand times before—as a welcome member of the church.

"CAREFUL, DEAR, I JUST MOPPED," SAID SHIRL, AS THE DOOR clicked shut behind me. Wiping her dishwater hands on her green apron, she looked as fresh and impeccable as ever. That was how someone had once described Shirl, "fresh and impeccable," and somehow in that moment the words found a way of looping in and out of my thoughts.

Despite the apparent kindness of her words, Shirl's expression was grim, and her long, salt-and-pepper hair gave her the look of the Wicked Witch of the West. She switched off the local news on the small kitchen television and took off her apron, folding it and placing it neatly on the granite countertop.

Fresh and impeccable as the wicked, wicked witch, I thought, but said nothing.

Shirl pulled her hair back into a tight ponytail as if she had heard my thoughts. "Are you hungry?" she asked. "I've made eggrolls." My stomach turned.

"You look terrible. I went out and bought you some Zicam for your sinuses. Go take it. It'll make you more comfortable. They're by the wipes," she said, gesturing to the small box of cold medicine that had been set next to the ever-present yellow container of Lysol wipes and green bottle of Germ-X on the counter between us.

I walked past her with my eyes on the floor, cowering like an abused pet. The heat from the oven and smell of the egg rolls made me suddenly nauseated. I recovered, and hesitated for a moment, imagining myself refusing the medicine in an act of courageous defiance. I grabbed the box and tore it open as I sat down on the bar stool at the counter.

"Here's a glass of water, hon."

I was already losing the battle.

I sat at the table and tried to calm my thoughts as we waited for the other church members to arrive. I took note of the white dry-erase board near the door. It simply read, LUKE,

BRUSH YOUR TEETH, a message to the youngest of their eleven children. On the grapevine-patterned wallpaper, my attention fell on a brown, wooden frame that contained the outline of a heart in the middle. Inside the heart were wooden figures with the names of Shirl's children painted in white on their chests. The figures were all suspended in a line on a thick gray wire. I had seen the framed figures a hundred times before, but they suddenly took on a new significance. I felt just like the little wooden girl on the wire—tied to my family, only ever allowed the freedom to move a centimeter in any direction.

It wasn't long before small groups of people began to arrive. Gramps and Gran were among the first, much to Shirl's surprise. Shirl's husband shuffled in soon after, tired from work, looking miserable to still be in his suit and tie. Marge followed in a women's dress suit, also fresh from work, seemingly just as put out by the timing of the event. Tim came in still wearing his uniform from the jail, where he was a captain. Other younger members, still in their teens, came in laughing and joking, apparently excited to witness the first intervention focusing on someone of their generation. Sara and Megan came in quietly and immediately took their seats. My parents were among the last to arrive. My dad had had time to change and looked relaxed in sweatpants and a T-shirt. My mom just looked exhausted.

None of them acknowledged my existence as they filed through the kitchen and into the game room. I'd spent countless hours in this room, doing homework, scrapbooking, playing board games, and playing rowdy games of Rock Band with Megan and other church friends. Being in choir, I was always eager to show off my singing chops, and regularly got a perfect score on vocals for Radiohead's "Creep," a song whose lyrics I found secretly empowering.

"WE'RE JUST ABOUT READY TO GO. LET'S GET THIS THING started," Shirl said, directing latecomers to a nearby row of black folding chairs. The rest had already taken their places on the cream-colored couches, which were arranged in a large U-shape. I took my seat at the bottom of the U, sharing the couch with my grandparents. Their nearness was comforting, and I was glad they had come after all. Shirl sat as close to me as she could on a couch perpendicular and to the left of mine. Her posture was predatory: rigidly erect, ready to pounce.

In the suspense of the final moments leading up to the intervention, I feared I was going to faint, or maybe lose control of my bladder. Standing strong as a united group, the WBC was unbelievably intimidating, at least to me. For them, the matter was beyond life and death—the repercussions of their judgment were eternal. It was shape up or, literally, go to hell.

I looked up at the gray atomic clock on the mustard yellow wall across from me. It was six forty-five. The meeting would start any moment. I wiped my clammy palms on my khaki work pants and held my breath, trying to steady my erratic breathing. My body ached with tension.

My watery eyes fell on a family picture taken at Ben's wedding eight years earlier. The picture had been in that same spot for years, but I felt like I was seeing it for the first time. All of us looked so young. I nearly grinned, remembering how it took nearly thirty minutes to get a picture where all the kids were both smiling and looking at the camera. I was there in the middle next to Sara, smiling too.

Someone coughed. I scanned the faces of the nearly thirty members in attendance, ranging in age from my sixteen-year-old cousin Grace to Gran, who had turned eighty-three in September. I recognized the people in the photos on the walls as members of my loving family, but the people in the room had taken on strange features, and in the surreal atmosphere of the moment, they were almost unrecognizable to me. My parents were standing in a corner by the door behind me and over my left shoulder. My dad was looking down at nothing in particular, lost in thought. My mom looked up and caught my gaze, giving me a smile of meek encouragement. Sara was sitting next to Marge on the next couch over from Shirl. Megan sat on the piano bench across the room, watching everything intently, looking almost as terrified as I felt.

"Libby, we brought you here today because we fear for your eternal soul," Shirl began, matter-of-factly, as if discussing the weather or the day's meal plan.

I nodded slowly, struggling to swallow.

"I know this started out because you were wearing a bikini," she continued, addressing me and the rest of the room at once, "but that's not the big issue. It's the way you reacted when you were questioned about wearing it."

"OK," I said, trying to get the words out quickly. "I told Megan I was sorry for how I reacted and I won't wear one again." I was too nervous to think of anything else. I looked back to Megan for some kind of reassurance. Her eyes flashed to her mother, and then down to her feet.

"OK, well," Shirl scoffed, "there's not much we can do about that subject. So moving on . . ."

"It seems as though you're always an arm's distance away," Brent added quietly, avoiding eye contact.

"I don't know what you mean by that," I said, though I knew exactly what he meant—that I wasn't helping out enough. I was stunned by the accusation, given the daily sacrifices I was required to make in the name of the church.

"It means you do just as much as you think is needed to keep off our radar," he said, finally looking at me.

"All right," was the only response I could summon. I wanted to remind them of all the times I tried to help, like when I wanted to help with the construction of the additions to a church member's house, only to be sent home by Shirl because she hadn't specifically requested my assistance. And what about all the days I had to miss work to babysit, file charts at the family law office, and paint their fences, or mow their lawns? I had spent my entire life in subservience to these people. I felt a small flail of belligerence inside myself.

In a moment of heavy silence, I tried to gauge the reactions of my other family members. My eyes kept falling on Marge, who was slumped low in her seat, looking down and shaking her head. My parents were also both looking down and offered no support. Part of me had hoped one of them would stand up in my defense, but I knew they wouldn't, for fear of severe retaliation. I felt guilty that they were in this position and that I had put them there. I knew I had let them down, and it broke my heart. It was one of the saddest moments of my life.

Megan was still looking at me anxiously. I could tell she was sorry I was going through this. But her mother had convinced her it was being done for my own good, that they were attempting to save my soul, so she did nothing, said nothing. It was then that I realized there was no one who would stand up for me—no one who could save me. I was truly alone.

"Maybe she's chaff," Tim chimed in, referring to a specific passage in the Bible. "Outwardly, it looks as though everything is fine, but deep down there's nothing there. There's no strength at the root. When the wind comes by, it will grab the chaff from the wheat and blow it away," he added, motioning with his hands. He was implying that I might not be one of God's elect, one of the few righteous souls deemed worthy of heaven. There was no doubt in their minds that they were the chosen people. And if I wasn't one of them, I was one of the condemned.

They spoke on without emotion, as if I wasn't even human. They spoke of me as if I were already an outcast, no longer part of the family. The veil of delusion under which I had been living began to lift once again. They claimed to model their lives after the love described in the Bible, though God's love, of course, was reserved only for them. Until that moment, I too had believed in that love, and was proud to be one of them, but now I felt what it was like to be on the other side of their love—the side of the hated and the damned.

After being disparaged by Shirl and the others, I was expected to address the church. Ben and two other members came around the couch behind me, leaned in close, and thrust their phones out in front of my face. There were members who couldn't attend the meeting, and they were on speakerphone, waiting to hear what I had to say. Ben held his blue Razr phone only inches from my face as a voice on the other end demanded I explain myself. The absurdity of the situation added to the feeling of being trapped in an unfolding nightmare. All the pressure from the anxiety, frustration, and humiliation I was suffering was almost unendurable. I felt I might scream or spontaneously combust.

"I want to help out more," I squeaked out through heavy sobs. They shook their heads and rolled their eyes. The phones were silent. Marge sneered.

There were so many things I could have said in my own defense. But I had learned from past interventions that any further refutation by me would only feed their fury.

Despite all the reservations I had about church beliefs, and how uncomfortable the community's actions made me at times, deep down I still wanted to please them—I wanted to belong. I was deathly afraid of the outside world, the world which I was told a member could never return from once they left. In that moment, I wanted another chance more than anything, but I couldn't find the words.

"I'm sorry," I added meekly, trying to find those magic words they all wanted to hear, to put things back the way they were.

Once my church family made up their minds, they never wavered, and it seemed pretty clear that Shirl and the others had all but made up their minds. I sat devastated, unable to do anything but cry. I was disappointed in my family, especially my parents, for not sticking up for me, but knew that they also feared, more than anything, the wrath of the church's contempt. Under Shirl's control, Megan was as helpless as I was. But I was surprised by Marge's disdain, considering her own pregnancy situation years earlier. I thought she of all people had to know what I was going through. But she judged me just as harshly as the others.

"Well . . . it sounds like everyone is mad at Lib," Gramps said simply, breaking the silence. I laughed through my tears at the obviousness of his statement.

"Do you think if there aren't as many people around, you'll be able to talk more?" Gran added.

"Yes," I said, still struggling to control my sobbing.

"Maybe we should stop here for now, and you can talk to smaller groups of people."

I smiled at her gratefully. "OK."

At seven thirty, Shirl announced the meeting was adjourned. The intervention had only lasted forty-five minutes, but it had felt like an eternity. I gave Gramps and Gran a big hug and thanked them for coming.

I walked with Megan into the kitchen, where she put her hand on my shoulder. "Libby, I know you can do this. You can change. If anyone can do this, you can." She sounded as if she was begging me.

"I know I can. I'll try."

We hugged, crying, and told each other we loved one another. I had never hugged anyone so tightly.

"She's too far gone," I heard Marge say from the other room.

I left dejected, without saying another word to anyone.

THE MORNING AFTER THE INTERVENTION, MY PHONE WOKE ME from a deep sleep. My alarm clock read six a.m. I looked at my phone and jumped out of bed—it was Shirl. I cleared my throat the best I could in hopes that she wouldn't accuse me of sleeping in; if Shirl was up, she expected everyone else to be up too. Still in a fog of sleep, I hesitated for as long as I could, but answered just before it went to voicemail.

"Hello?" I croaked. My voice had betrayed me; I was mortified.

"Libby?"

"Yes," I answered, finding my voice.

"Did you get that email I sent last night?" Shirl asked, sounding impatient already.

"I'm getting my laptop right now and I can look for it," I responded, full of dread. I hadn't seen it, and could only imagine what might be in it. I waited for my computer to boot up, which seemed to be taking longer than it ever had before.

"All right," she continued. "I know that during the day you don't work, but instead you're frolicking about. And when you claimed to have a school internship for physical therapy in Joplin, you were messing around with things you ought not to be."

I opened the email and began to read it. My mouth fell open in astonishment as my eyes scanned over page after page of all-caps Bible quotations accompanied by frantic, nearly incomprehensible ranting. In among all the yelling and quoting of scripture, Shirl accused my mother of raising her children under a false doctrine—my mom, Shirl claimed, wasn't raising her children to believe in and follow the God of the Bible. She also chastised my dad for permitting my mom to raise us this way. She told my mom that she had raised us to hate everyone at the WBC; that they were not worthy of our time and efforts. "LIBBY IS IN PERIL!! BETTY IS IN PERIL!! WE ARE IN PERIL!!" the email screamed. She again brought up the 4B rule, accused me of lying about how I got the bikinis, and demanded we all "FIX THIS AND GO FORWARD!!"

Part of the email was addressed directly to me:

"Libby—put away that maudlin squally crap. BUCK UP!! It is time for you to decide—are you a servant of God OR NOT!! If so, put away this crap. BRING FORTH FRUIT that is meet for repentance! THAT must be said for Fred and Betty. I have great hope for Fred Jr. because he IS tenderhearted toward the servants of God and because he IS and HAS BEEN faithful all these years. Betty—you have provoked your children to wrath. You have brought sorrow upon your house that is NEEDLESS because of this false doctrine. We have people sitting around worried about how you will respond to all this. It is TIME for YOU Betty to make sure that people KNOW that it is well with you!! Frankly, our response to all these questions from this generation about—WHAT ABOUT THE FEELINGS OF THE REBELS!? YIKES!!!!!!!!!!!!!!!!!!!!!!!!! So we must do that as well????????????????? Right now I feel outraged!! Right now I feel VERY scared for us—for all of us!!!!!!!!!!! This must GO AWAY!! FOREVER!!

"I love you all!! Please!!!!!!!"

I had no idea how to respond to this.

"Why did your family go to Puerto Rico for your family vacation?" Shirl demanded while I was still trying to digest the histrionic rant. "We're not legally able to picket there, so why did you go there? I would never go anywhere I couldn't picket."

In a moment of bravery, I defended myself. "It wasn't my idea to go to Puerto Rico. It was Sara's. I wanted to go to Texas," I told her truthfully. I also wanted to remind her of how her husband had so enthusiastically recommended Puerto Rico, and tell her that I'd noticed how she treated every picket like a vacation and rarely came out for ones closer to home. I said nothing, still scanning the email in disbelief.

"You know Sharon is now a drug addict and a drunk, and that's how you'll end up if you leave," she added, never missing a chance to bring up my disinherited older sister.

"OK . . ." I said vaguely. Reading the email while listening to Shirl's relentless invective, I suddenly questioned her sanity. And if her sanity was in question, the entire church's was also suspect. I had been raised to believe the church was full of honest, hardworking, pious individuals—God's chosen elect. But despite years of conditioning, it was becoming clear to me that there was something very wrong with the way these people were behaving. Something was rotten at the core.

"You started working behind my back on Gramps to get both Gramps and Gran on your side." Her voice was more spiteful than ever.

"Actually, I've been working on his back for a few weeks now. You can ask him," I retorted, growing braver and more fed up with her accusations.

145

"Well," she said, "if you leave, you can never come back." This wasn't the first time she'd said this to me.

I stayed silent.

"If you're not going to say anything, then I guess this conversation is over," she said, disgusted. She hung up.

I got ready for work, still struggling to process all that had just happened. I felt betrayed, like I'd been living a lie, and was slowly and painfully waking up to the truth. Through the facade of faithfulness, the mask of self-righteousness, the WBC's true face was beginning to show.

THE DAYS FOLLOWING THE INTERVENTION WERE THE MOST stressful of my life. I tried my best to continue on, but in everything I did, I could feel the suspicious eyes of the church watching over my shoulder. Everywhere I went, I felt surrounded by a cloud of judgment and condemnation. I had lived with that paranoia my entire life: the constant sense of being watched, the fear that if I so much as had a bad thought about my family, they would somehow find out. But in those final days, the feeling had grown so intense that it was painfully visceral.

I felt I was being persecuted, the target of a never-ending stream of ridiculous accusations and unreasonable demands. More than anything, I felt trapped. But I still couldn't see myself walking away from the church, leaving my family. The unknown world outside was too dangerous, too frightening. I feared for my soul. I had had the fear of hell drummed into me for as long as I could remember, and was reminded daily that eternal damnation lay in wait for the entire world outside of the church walls. The thought of leaving the church was always accompanied by images of fire pouring from my eyes and an eternity of weeping, wailing, and gnashing of teeth, gnawing my tongue in excruciating pain. There was no way out. I fell into a deep depression, and spent most of my downtime at work crying in the basement.

The physical therapy office I worked at in Eudora, forty-five minutes from home, was my only place of relative escape. Some members of the church didn't like that the office was so far from home, but I was grateful to be able to put some distance between the tumultuous church and myself. This didn't stop them, after the intervention, from barraging my cell phone with voicemails and text messages demanding that I quit my job and find another place to work closer to home. Other members, including Brent, were allowed to commute to work. I liked working in Eudora, had worked hard to get where I was, and felt their demands represented an unfair double standard. I refused to consider leaving my job. They wanted to control me as much as possible. It seemed no matter the sacrifices I made, they would never be satisfied. I ignored their messages.

I HAPPENED TO BE CHECKING MY PHONE WHEN GRAMPS called. I had no idea it would be the last time I would speak to him.

"How are you doing, hon?" he asked.

"I'm fine," I replied, fighting back tears.

"You're not thinking of leaving, are you?" he asked.

"No," I said. In the moment, I was telling the truth. The fear of the outside world, of damnation, was still too powerful. It had nothing to offer but disease, sorrow, heartache, sadness, drugs, and alcohol.

"I'm glad to hear that. Remember that I love you," he said softly.

"I love you, too," I said, forcing a steady voice as tears streamed down my cheeks.

I hung up the phone and immediately thought of Megan. In that moment, I realized I couldn't stay. She and Gramps seemed to be the only ones who wanted anything to do with me. We had been as close as sisters our entire lives. I wished I could talk her into leaving with me, but I was on my own. There was no middle ground. By pushing me away, treating me like an outcast within my own family, they were forcing me to make a drastic decision.

I thought about Sharon, who had left more than ten years ago. From the stories I heard, her life was a complete mess. Over the years, my mom had taken multiple phone calls from bill collectors because she wasn't paying her bills. Church members also talked regularly about how she had been abusing drugs and alcohol. Shirl used stories of my sister's misery and hardship to keep me scared, keep me close. She wanted me to believe I was no different from Sharon, that I'd fall into the same fate. I wondered if the stories were true, or if they would make up similar stories about me.

I NEEDED TO TALK THINGS THROUGH WITH SOMEONE I TRUSTED. I turned to my coworker Meg for help. Meg and I were close in age, and she was always friendly to me at work. I considered her a friend—though, like the friends I had at school growing up, our friendship had limits prescribed by the church: you were never supposed to get too close to someone outside WBC. After all that had happened, I felt she was the only one left I could trust. I approached Meg at her work desk and blurted out what had happened—as is my style, especially when I'm anxious—and said that I was thinking about leaving the church.

She turned her office chair away from her computer to see me leaning against the counter overlooking her desk. "What's been keeping you from leaving?" she asked. She looked concerned. My face clearly showed how torn up I was inside.

"I don't want to go to hell!" I exclaimed in terror, feeling like a volcano about to erupt. Images of fiery eyes and gnashing teeth came rushing back. Never in my wildest dreams had I thought I could confide my biggest fear to someone outside of the church. But the fear had been building up inside me for so long that I simply couldn't contain it any longer.

"I think the only reason you're staying there is because that's all you've ever known. It's how you were raised. It's your lifestyle," Meg observed. Her words were simple—obvious, even. But hearing them in that moment flipped a switch for me, and suddenly everything I had ever known came into question.

"Yeah," I replied nervously, too stunned by the honest power of my thoughts to say more. A wave of relief washed over me. My parents raised me to express little or no emotion, and I had just confessed my biggest fear to someone I barely knew. I was sick of the constant paranoia and the unending anxiety. I suddenly realized why the church had been so adamant about keeping us from spending time with friends outside of the church. They wanted me to have as little contact as possible with anyone who might question what the WBC was doing—what I was doing. They figured as long as they kept me contained, I wouldn't have cause to question my surroundings, to question their authority. But they had gone too far.

"Do you think I should move out?" I had all but made up my mind, but still valued her opinion, and I wanted to hear her say it. It was the biggest decision of my life.

"You should do what you want. I'll help any way I can."

"I don't know how to live, though. I mean—I don't know the process to pay bills—I don't have a place to stay. What will I do with my mail? And last year's tax information? And I'll need my birth certificate . . ." I rambled anxiously, fidgeting with the Kleenex box on the counter and restlessly kicking my shoes into the carpet.

"You'll figure it all out," Meg answered calmly. "Everyone does. Just ask questions to the right people. You can forward your mail to my place if you want."

"OK. Thanks! That will help a lot." I shook my head in disbelief. "I can't believe I'm actually considering this. I don't know what to do!"

"Well," she said, "do you think this will be the best for you? That's all you need to think about. Do what you think is best for you."

This was the first time anyone ever asked me to think of myself, to do what was best for me. I had always been told that every thought, every action, had to be for the betterment of the church, for the satisfaction of the elders. Meg's comment awoke a courage hiding deep within me. Thinking of my own well-being, if only for a few moments, felt alien, like I was committing a dreadful sin, but also extremely liberating.

I can do this. I have to do this. A lightning bolt of clarity hit me all at once. I suddenly and desperately needed to get out. I now had no doubt I needed to leave the church and start a new life. After almost twenty-six years of being brainwashed into conformity, it was time I started thinking for myself and doing what was right for me. I knew if I stayed, I'd lose myself completely. Meg's words of careful encouragement gave me hope for the future, and strength enough to take the next step forward.

THE FIRST THING I HAD TO DO WAS CALL A COUPLE OF PATIENTS to ask if they would reschedule their appointments for later that day. They agreed, buying me what I hoped would be enough time to make the forty-five-minute drive to Topeka, get my stuff, and drive all the way back to Eudora.

Meg and I jumped in my Honda Civic and headed for the highway. As we pulled onto the interstate, my phone rang— it was my dad. I knew there was no way of talking to him without Shirl and the rest of the church hearing about it; he wouldn't understand what I was doing any more than they would. Part of me was also afraid that if I heard the soothing tone he had used to calm me down so many times in the past, I might change my mind. Seeing my turmoil, Meg gave me a look of reassurance. It rang one last time and went to voicemail.

He left a message, saying he hoped I was having a good day. He reassured me that everything would work out; all I needed to do was talk to people in the church, and we would be able to resolve their concerns. I knew that wasn't true. I loved my dad dearly, and still do. The regret of not answering that call is something I'll always carry with me. We have not spoken since.

I continued driving. Every mile marker felt hours apart. I squinted against the glare of the sun, which was still high in the wide Kansas sky. The skin on my left arm and the back of my neck reddened from the unseasonable warmth of the afternoon, and I broke into a sweat. It was only mid-March, but in my state of near-panic, the heat was almost unbearable. I noticed the tenseness of my arms and shoulders, and tried to shake it off. Turning on the air conditioning and then the stereo, I searched for a distraction.

"And the feeling coming from my bones, it says find a home," Jack White sang over a screeching electric guitar.

JUST OUTSIDE OF TOPEKA, I CALLED MY FRIEND CAROL, WHO was working at the Topeka branch of the company I worked for. Carol was my boss, but I had befriended her and another woman, Faith, at the office while finishing up my last round of clinicals before getting my degree. Their office was near my house, and I was hoping that with their help, and a couple of extra cars, I would be able to get most of the possessions I needed from the house. Hearing the urgency in my voice, they agreed to drop what they were doing to help.

Reaching Topeka, I took the Gage Street exit mechanically, still in a haze. Except for the terrible butterflies in my stomach, I felt completely numb.

"What if I get in trouble for wearing jeans?" Meg asked as we passed Gage Park, the place where the picketing began. Carol had recently sent a message to all employees about proper workplace attire; wearing jeans was no longer allowed.

"Meg!" I couldn't help but laugh. "I think your choice in pants will be the last thing on Carol's mind." I was grateful for the distraction, and the rare moment to get out of my own head and catch my breath.

I pulled up to the Topeka branch and ran inside to fetch Carol and Faith. We were in our cars ready to go moments later. Carol followed me in her Prius, with Faith right behind.

We wound our way through the busy shopping center where the office was located and through the surrounding middle-class neighborhoods, passing several sites that we picketed frequently. As I turned each corner, I feared I might come upon a picket in progress. Any member of the church would recognize my car and know something was wrong. I held my breath as I turned onto Holly Lane, and my house came into view.

I knew my immediate family would be out of town at a picket, my parents in Illinois and Sara in Massachusetts, but we were only half a mile from the church, and as paranoid and protective as the church was, it was likely that Shirl or another member would come by to check up. Given everything that had unfolded in the past few days, they were also no doubt suspicious that I might try to leave, and if Shirl had the chance to catch me in the act, she would. If she did, she would likely do more than just a lot of yelling. I was certain she'd cause a scene, but it also wouldn't have surprised me if she called the police to try to file charges for trespassing since my parents were away and I didn't own the house.

WE PULLED UP IN FRONT OF THE HOUSE AND QUICKLY GATHERED at the door. My hands shook as I pushed it open. We stepped inside. *OK, now what?* I thought. Time was short—I needed a game plan.

"We only have a few minutes to get this done. Follow me," I said to the girls as we walked.

I gave Meg, Carol, and Faith a quick rundown of the layout of the house as they followed me toward the back staircase that led to my room. Having always separated my personal and professional lives, it was strange welcoming people from the outside world into my house, people who I knew were unwelcome by the church. But despite everything I'd been told, I knew there were good people in the outside world, and it was these good people who stood by me in my hour of greatest need.

They followed me into my room. My bedroom, with its dark-pink carpet, big bright windows, and light-pink walls, had often served as a safe place where I could take refuge from the turmoil of church life. But it was a sanctuary only while I was in it. Personal space and privacy were ridiculous notions to Shirl and the other church members, and I had always been too afraid to keep a diary or journal, for fear someone would take it and read it.

The girls stood just inside the doorway, awaiting instruction. "I mostly need my clothes and shoes," I told them. "I want the pictures with their frames and everything off the shelves. I also need my schoolbooks," I added, motioning toward the objects as I listed them.

"We can use the bedspread to wrap up the clothes. That way we can carry them all at once," Carol suggested.

"Great! Use the bedspread . . . and this blanket for the rest." I replied, grabbing a pink Hello Kitty throw blanket and laying it out flat onto the carpet.

The girls got to work, grabbing clothes from the closets and drawers as I hastily scanned the rest of the room. I was doing my best to be conscious of taking only what was mine, which meant leaving the new shoes my mom had bought me a few days before. As a member of the church, I, like all the others, had always been provided for, spoiled even, and I honestly didn't feel like any of it belonged to me. It wasn't until later that I'd notice that the security and spoils of church life had always been designed to keep me in comfortable complacency. I was terrified of moving out into the unknown world, but I knew the time had come to create my own life.

I emptied my green pillowcases of their pillows and began shoving framed family pictures and other smaller belongings into them. I threw my schoolbooks and other notebooks, along with my high school yearbooks and a Bible, into a lavender backpack.

"OK?" asked Meg, referring to the two large piles of clothing on the blankets.

"Perfect. Now we can take everything downstairs and leave it by the door. After we've got it all there, we'll run to the cars and pack them as quickly as we can. I don't want to cause a big scene."

"Why did I wear these high heels?" Faith exclaimed, as she stumbled down the stairs, laughing.

Carol paused a moment to wipe the sweat off of her brow. "And why, out of all days, did I choose to wear a cashmere sweater—it's hot!" she added, as she tried to roll up her sleeves, only to have the limp fabric fall back down to her wrists.

I was extremely grateful for the girls—for their help, and their distractions. I was still in a state of disbelief about what I was doing. The feelings of almost overwhelming doubt and dread wouldn't subside. But in my panicked state, the girls offered a much-needed dose of humility and humor. I'm sure they were as nervous as I was. We had no way of knowing if someone was about to walk through the door to try to stop us. They were willing to take that risk and, like true friends, were ready to support me and my choice to escape from the church any way they could.

"Do you think anyone will come and try to stop us?" Meg asked.

"I don't think so, but let's hurry up just in case," I said.

The last items to go down the stairs were the biggest: my turquoise papasan chair, a small dresser with multicolored drawers where I kept many of my most sentimental possessions, a black bookshelf, and a small lingerie chest I could use to store my clothes. Working together, we were able to get these down the stairs and to the front door.

After several frenzied trips through the house, we had everything piled in the entryway, ready to go—nearly twenty-six years packed in thirty minutes. We rested for a moment, trying to figure out how we would fit everything into the cars.

"Let's take the chair and the other furniture out first, and we can pack my clothes and everything else around them," I said, then stopped as I realized a car was coming down the street. I didn't recognize it and let out a sigh of relief. As I watched it turn the corner, a wave of excitement struck me, despite all the stress. I opened the door and stood for a moment, drenched in sunlight. A new life sat waiting for me in the form of three empty cars, only a few yards away.

Once we got as many of my belongings as we could fit into the cars, the girls agreed to wait while I went back up to my room for one final look. I had been moving as if in a dream, still half convinced I would wake up to find it hadn't happened at all. The only way to maintain my sanity was to disconnect, to not think about the magnitude of what I was doing, or all of the heartbreaking consequences I would soon face. Even in that state of shock, I knew I was doing what had to be done, though it meant leaving everyone and everything behind—all at once and with no good-byes.

As I turned to leave, I got a text message from my mom asking how my day was going. I wanted so badly to respond, to tell her I wasn't having a good day, I was in fact leaving her forever. I wanted to tell her one last time that I loved her. But I couldn't. A clean break might somehow make it easier, lessen the pain for everyone. I threw the phone on the bed, and shut the door behind me.

THE DAY I MOVED OUT WAS SIMULTANEOUSLY THE MOST joyful and most traumatic day of my life. I knew I would never see my family again. But they forced me to make a choice between a life of servitude under the strict rule of the church—a life lived in fear, paranoia, hatred, and hostility—and a life that was unknown, uncertain, but one of my own making. For them, faith meant slavery to the church and to their hypocritical ideals of love and loyalty to God. But somehow, by some power, I had found a greater kind of faith. I was walking the tightrope between faith and freedom, with no end in sight. It was time to cut the wire.

CHAPTER SIX

A DIFFICULT ADJUSTMENT, AND FINDING LOVE

As Meg and I pulled our cars away from the curb, I felt like I was in a dream. "I can't believe I'm doing this," I said out loud, to no one. "I can't believe it." I thought about the pair of shoes I'd left on my bed, a new pair of sandals my mom had just bought me. It was too late to go back and get them. She'd think I didn't like them, that I was ungrateful for her having given them to me in the first place. So stupid of me. I couldn't stop thinking about it. It was the last gift she had given me. Nausea welled up in me as I imagined my family finding out I was gone. I rolled down the window, wondering if I might actually throw up.

As we rounded the corner, I kept a lookout for family members walking along the sidewalk in the neighborhood. Would I see Shirl? She seemed to know everything and be everywhere—maybe she had somehow found out about my plan? Or what about my uncle Charles, who lived across the street from us and worked from home? What if I was spotted?

What if someone came after me and tried to stop me? Would I have the strength to still go through with it? I already missed the comfort of being there. I didn't know if I'd be able to resist the pull of someone actually coming after me to bring me home.

But no one did. The streets were quiet. As we pulled onto the highway, I realized I was free. I mulled that word over with a heavy heart. I didn't feel liberated; I was terrified and achingly sad. I might never see my parents again. The thought stabbed into my gut like a knife.

Another even more horrifying thought gnawed away at me, looming larger than even losing my family: I'd just given up my chance at eternal paradise. Once I made the choice to reject the church and join the rest of the world, I became a worker of iniquity—doomed to spend my afterlife brutally tormented with fire and brimstone in hell, my face full of flames and worms forever eating away at me. Was it really worth it to prove my point in this world to suffer so much in the next? I could only imagine what would be said about me at the next church service. I was *anathema maranatha*, guilty of the worst crime in the Bible: knowingly turning my back on God. And Gramps had tried so hard to get me into heaven.

IN LAWRENCE, ABOUT A HALF HOUR AWAY, I MOVED MY CARFUL of belongings into a colleague's spare room. He had agreed to this arrangement that day, but didn't seem all that happy to actually see me when I showed up at his small white house. He hung around in the living room as I hurried back and forth carrying what was left of my life, clumsily opening and shutting the chained gate outside with every trip. Once I had everything unloaded, Meg asked if I wanted her to stay. "No, thanks, I'll be fine," I said with a big smile, grateful for years of training on how to seem like everything was OK even when you were falling apart inside. I drove her home and waved as I pulled away. After returning to my temporary shelter, I retreated to the small room I had filled up and closed the door partway, not wanting to be rude by shutting it all the way.

This was crazy. What had I done? What on earth was I going to do? My coworkers had made me think I was capable of taking care of myself, but faced with the reality of it, I began to suspect they were wrong. How could you go from a life where everything was taken care of for you to knowing how to live on your own?

I sat on a crate and stared blankly, letting the numbness take over. At least I didn't have to pretend to be cheerful in here. The smell of incense drifted in from the living room. Patchouli. Maybe my massage therapist friend had intended it to be comforting, but I found it sort of awful. I closed the door all the way, as softly as I could, and continued to sit and stare.

At night, I curled up in a blanket on the couch in the living room. I turned off the light but I couldn't turn off my brain, which circled back endlessly to one thought: I was likely never going to see my parents again. I hadn't even had a chance to say good-bye. For the first time since we'd set out to get my things, I let myself give in to tears. Eventually, I tired myself out from crying enough to fall asleep for a few hours.

When I woke up, I realized it was Saturday. I had moved out of my house on Friday the thirteenth, as it happened. A whole weekend stretched out in front of me, planless. At home, this would have been unthinkable; there was always a way to use your time productively for the good of the church, even if it was just a few minutes in between other tasks. I had no idea what to do with myself. Desperate to keep busy, I called my boss, Carol, on the pretext of checking in to see if she needed any help. She saw through me, though.

"Are you OK?" she asked. "Why don't you move in over here instead, for the time being?" She insisted, and I accepted gratefully. If I stayed here, I was just going to barricade myself in that storage room and ruminate on how I'd ruined my life and was headed straight for hell.

As it turned out, that was mostly what I did at my boss's house too, except that she lived in a mansion with a swimming pool in the backyard. It was very luxurious, but I spent the majority of those first weeks there in a spare bedroom on the second floor. I worked as much as I possibly could. At my family's insistence, I had always worked four days a week instead of five, so as to have a weekday to devote to the church—babysitting, cleaning, helping out at the law office. Now I picked up shifts for a fifth day too, and was grateful for the mental distraction.

"You're doing so well!" coworkers kept telling me. Everyone was very encouraging and I didn't want to let them down; the last thing I needed was to make a spectacle of myself. So I kept my loneliness and sadness to myself, put on a smile, and pretended everything was fine. When work was over, though, I was forced to deal with my own thoughts.

I didn't miss the daily Bible discussions in the evenings, or the long sermons at church on Sunday. But I desperately missed the routine, and my family. What was Megan doing right now? Or Sara? Were they all talking about me? Had they been told never to talk to me again?

I became obsessed with the thought that I needed to buy my own house, though I didn't really know how I'd go about doing that. So I began by buying random kitchen items: a dish towel, a spatula. It felt like preparation. I didn't know how to think bigger than that.

At the same time, I lived in constant fear that I wouldn't need any of my preparations, because the world was probably going to end. My family had been saying this with increasing frequency in the months before I left—that the signs of the time indicated the Lord would be returning within the next couple of years. Now, I would walk down the street and suddenly be gripped by panic that something terrible was going to happen to me, as punishment for leaving the only true Church of the Lord Jesus Christ. When I'd been a Westboro member, I'd been taught to be happy about anything bad that happened in the world, as this was just more evidence the Lord would be returning soon. Now that I was on the outside, I felt terror at what might become of me when the day of reckoning was at hand.

SEVERAL DAYS AFTER LEAVING, I EMAILED MY MOTHER. KEEPING my note as brief and impersonal as possible—despite feeling desperate to tell her how sorry I was and how much I missed her and my dad and Sara—I told her I intended to pay her and my sister back as soon as I could for the loan they'd given me to buy my new car. As it turned out, she forwarded that email to Shirl, who wrote back on my mother's behalf.

"Your mom, dad, and Sara would prefer that you not communicate with them directly. They asked me to address unresolved issues with you," she wrote. "About the car: they are not willing to carry your loan, we must not be encumbered with the cares of this life." It was such a Shirl thing to say. She went on to instruct me to immediately take out a loan for the full amount I owed them—over $13,000.

Busy with work, and my own depression, I ignored my email inbox for several days, and the message sat there unread. In the meantime, incensed that I hadn't written back right away, Shirl had flown into action, assigning someone in the church—I still don't know who—to come and take my car. My parents had had an extra key to my new Honda Civic hybrid, so I knew that's how it had happened.

One afternoon, at my PT office, I looked out the window and realized the car was missing. I was with a patient, so I kept my sense of alarm to myself and went on working. As soon as he'd left, I got onto the computer and checked my email, seeing Shirl's blast of rage for the first time. In addition to all the invective, she'd told me I needed to put the car and insurance in my name only. After I'd done this, she said, she would consider giving the car back—but she'd have to see how she felt at the time.

Frustrated but not all that surprised at this turn of events, I switched the title and arranged for a friend to bring the paperwork to Shirl as proof, and to pick up my car. But it wasn't that easy; Shirl wouldn't allow a third party to be involved, turning my friend away with a curt, "Tell Libby she'll need to deal with me directly." I decided, instead, to call the police and report the car as stolen. They believed me—they were familiar with the antics of Westboro, and most of them viewed the church as a nuisance. They escorted me and two of my coworkers, Brandon and Faith, to Shirl's house to get the car. The police handled all the interaction while I stayed in the car, slouching down as low as possible in the back seat to avoid being seen or, worse, having to see my immediate family. But I wanted to know anyway.

"What's going on? What's going on?" I asked Brandon. "It looks like a swarm of ants," he said, uncomfortably laughing while describing the way my family members were coming out of their houses to investigate, video cameras running, yelling to one another. I had expected nothing less from my family, of course, but I could tell Brandon was a little stunned by the intensity of the scene. "Here they come with their cameras," he warned.

I slumped down even further. "We need to move," I said. "Drive to the first stop sign and turn right. Park on the side of the road." What was I so afraid of? That they would try to talk me into coming back? That they wouldn't? We waited silently for the police to call me, which they did less than five minutes later. They arranged to meet us at a nearby McDonald's, telling me that Shirl had initially lied to them, saying she had no idea what car they were talking about. The cop rolled his eyes as he described his conversation with her, and boy, did I understand where he was coming from. "They have their cameras, but we have our cameras, too," he said. "We'll get you your car back." Five hours later, I was back in my car. The cops had told me they'd get a search warrant from the attorney general if Shirl didn't comply, and being a lawyer, I guess she knew when she was beaten.

EMBOLDENED AFTER HAVING BEATEN SHIRL THIS ONE TIME, I tried to open myself up to as many new experiences as possible. One April night I went to Brandon's house with several of his friends to have dinner and watch a movie. An evening activity like this would have been virtually unheard of before; it would have immediately stirred up suspicion that I was "doing things I ought not to be," as Shirl had put it so many times.

My head spun as I drove to Brandon's, and I realized I was wearing my glasses and my contact lenses simultaneously. I breathed a sigh of relief, because I'd thought for a minute my eyesight was going in addition to everything else in my life falling apart.

Brandon cooked dinner and we all watched an animated Disney movie. I felt comfortable enough with him and the others to lie slumped on the sofa, which was new for me. I was used to feeling so awkward and formal around other people—anyone who wasn't a relative, really—that I'd sit ramrod-straight. At one point, one of the other girls there did a shot of liquor. I knew *that* was something I wasn't remotely ready for.

WHEN MY BIRTHDAY ROLLED AROUND A MONTH AFTER LEAVING, I figured I'd just pretend it wasn't happening. Since my family had never celebrated individual birthdays, I wasn't in the habit of doing it anyway. But that morning when I arrived at the physical therapy office, Meg and Brandon had filled the clinic with balloons. Brandon peeked through the doorway, a cake in his hands, followed by Meg.

"Happy birthday," they said quietly, rather than shouting. "We didn't want to startle you by hiding in here or yelling," Meg added. I laughed, which came out as more of a croak due to the cold I'd been nursing, then started to cry in spite of myself. I'd always wanted a surprise party.

On the table was a hilariously oversized birthday card. When I opened it, it played Reel 2 Real's "I Like to Move It," which made me laugh more. Brandon put down the cake, which he'd made from scratch, and dished out three slices on paper plates. He handed me a gift bag, and I unwrapped the tissue paper around a can opener.

"We know you're buying stuff for a new place," he said, awkwardly but kindly. It was an odd gift, but they really did get it; they knew I was in a strange place, and that can opener was a sweet show of support.

That afternoon, they took me to Maurice's to go shopping for new clothes, as I'd left a lot of mine behind. I had always loved shopping with my sister and cousins, and I felt out of place doing it with anyone but them. It felt strange and wrong and liberating to be able to try on anything I wanted, without fear of Shirl thinking it was too revealing, without having to put it to the 4B test. "Are you guys sure you want to be doing this?" I kept asking Brandon and Meg. I felt like I was a burden, like my learning curve for life was so slow, they must be bored with this kind of thing. But they assured me it was fine, that I was doing fine.

As nice as my coworkers were, I still didn't quite believe they thought of me as a friend. I had only ever really relied on my family for friendship. And now I couldn't talk to any of them. But I needed to connect with someone about what was going on, and I didn't want to overburden my coworkers. So I did what seemed natural at the time: I called a Kansas City radio station, 96.5, The Buzz. We used to call them all the time to request songs—and to also tell them they were going to hell.

They were glad to hear from me, and put me on with a DJ named Lazlo I'd talked to frequently. We set up a time for me to talk with him on the air that afternoon. I told him I'd left the church—it felt strange not to be lecturing him about God's wrath. He said he was proud of me for leaving. He didn't expect an apology for all the mean things I'd said over the years; he seemed genuinely happy for me that I had gotten out. He asked why I'd done it and I told him about the bikini.

"I know that sounds stupid and trivial," I said, "but it wasn't about the bikini, really. It was the way they treated me." He said he was really proud of me again and asked if I needed any help or any money. I laughed and said no. As we talked, I thought about how often we'd listened to this station and wondered if maybe it was a way to at least let my family know I was OK. Megan and Jael always listened to this station; perhaps they'd hear this and realize I was still the same Libby I'd always been, that I hadn't been swallowed up or corrupted or instantly changed by the evils of the outside world.

I didn't take any money from the station, but I did say yes to Lazlo's offer of concert tickets, to a show at the Midland Theater in Kansas City. It was the first rock concert I'd ever been to, some local band I'd never heard of. I took a female patient of mine who'd become a friend, and I wore a dress I'd bought in Puerto Rico but had always been too scared to actually wear in public. It was silky, black and gold, and had a slit all the way down to the belly button. "I like your dress!" said a woman standing next to me at the show. "Thank you!" I said. "I've never worn anything like it before!" We were in the front row, and I had a great time. I danced and laughed with my friend and with complete strangers. I loved the rock band, with its long-haired lead singer. My mind flitted only occasionally to how disgusted my family would have been at my behavior; I'd truly joined the ranks of the fallen.

ONE OF THE FORBIDDEN THINGS I WAS THE MOST EXCITED — and terrified—to do was cut my hair. I'd thought about it for years, what it would be like not to have the weight of the locks that went down past my rear end. It was a sensation I'd never have known staying in the church, but now I had cut myself free, so it seemed like a good time to get a literal cut, too. My whole life I had been defined by my hair, to some extent; it was the thing that made all of us stand out in Topeka. To alter it would be a definitive move forward. Was I ready?

I chose a salon in Lawrence called Dash, which my coworkers had told me was a nice place with friendly haircutters. When the appointment time neared, my feelings of nervousness intensified. While I waited in the lobby, I found myself tearing at my thumb's cuticle, like I did whenever I was anxious about something.

The woman they'd assigned me had dyed blonde hair and lots of makeup on; she clearly spent a lot of time on her looks. When I told her it was my first-ever haircut, her blue-shadowed eyes widened.

"Wow," she said. "That's cool!" I sat down in the chair and explained that I still wanted long hair—just not THAT long. I figured maybe it wouldn't be quite so blasphemous if I still kept my hair in more or less the same style. Maybe God wouldn't mind quite so much about taking off a few inches. I rattled on about whatever I could think of while she got to work, talking a mile a minute like I always did when I was nervous. She ended up cutting off about a foot of the length, which lay all around me on the floor. I didn't know back then that you could donate hair for wigs, so I just left it there.

"This is crazy," I kept saying as she worked away. "I can't believe I'm doing this." By the time she was done, my hair hung just below my shoulders, looking much fuller than I'd ever seen it before. I reached up and touched the ends. They felt so soft! I felt truly, terrifyingly free at that moment; there was really no going back now. I had been told my entire life that my hair was my "glory." And I had just left a good part of it on a salon floor. My departure from the church was complete.

Tears formed, but I managed not to break down. Meg, who'd been standing by me during the cut, smiled encouragingly. "It looks great!" she said. Before we left, I snapped a picture of the piles of brown hair I'd left around the chair.

SHORTLY AFTER THAT, BRANDON AND I WERE SHOPPING ON Massachusetts Street, one of the main drags in Lawrence, and had just entered Urban Outfitters when I saw a familiar face. It was a strikingly handsome young guy with short dark hair, sitting on a bench inside with a friend. Our eyes met and I flashed back to why he looked familiar.

The summer before, he had come into my physical therapy practice. My boss had seen him initially, but had assigned me to treat him when he came back in. Since I had just started practicing on my own—I was no longer a student with a clinical instructor to fall back on—I was a little nervous. I hadn't seen many patients on my own at that point. I stood at the front desk looking over his chart, trying to make sense of my boss's chicken-scratch writing. I could make out that something was wrong with his left pinky, and that was about it.

The young man walked into the lobby, and I immediately noted how good-looking he was, so much so that I blushed in spite of myself. He had an easy, blinding-white smile and beautiful dark skin. He was dressed like a typical Kansas guy, in an athletic shirt and cargo shorts. "I'm Logan Alvarez," he said. "I'm here for my two o'clock appointment." I smiled back, introduced myself, and asked him to sit down. When I turned to the counter to get his chart, my eyes flicked to his date of birth: He was only seventeen, more than seven years younger than me! I couldn't believe it; he seemed like he was my age, not at all like a teenager.

I called Logan back to the tiny treatment room, the last door at the back of the small three-room office. I admitted that I couldn't really read my boss's writing, and asked what exactly was wrong, and what she'd done the last time he was there. He'd hurt his finger playing football, he told me, and she'd treated it initially with underwater ultrasound.

Great—a treatment I'd never done before. Not only did I have to do something for the first time, but I was already flustered because he was so cute. Luckily, underwater ultrasound isn't very tricky, so I managed to pull it off without looking too awkward.

The next part was harder for me, though: I had to manually stretch all the joints and perform joint mobilizations to his left pinky because it was stuck in the flexed position. This amounted to holding his left hand in both of my hands. I tried to concentrate on being professional and not on looking into his gorgeous brown eyes. We joked around easily, and I felt myself relaxing. He told me about the college parties he went to with his older brothers, full of drinking and debauchery. I wasn't impressed, and I told him so. He didn't seem to mind. I concluded the treatment by dipping his hand in paraffin, and we chatted more during the ten minutes he had to let it set. He told me about his family, and I deliberately did not tell him about mine. I figured he probably knew who I was, though, given my last name.

After a few weeks, he stopped coming for treatments, missing his last week altogether. I was disappointed not to see him anymore, but reasoned that this was just part of the PT business—meeting clients you liked and then having them drop out of your life again.

So when I saw him outside the Urban Outfitters, my heart soared. I was surprised by how thrilled I was to see him. I had an easy conversation starter: I walked over to the benches and mock-scolded him, "You missed your last visit!" I worried for a second he might not recognize me with my new, shorter hair. But his eyes lit up. "I meant to come by!" he apologized. So I told him he could come in whenever he wanted.

Sure enough, the very next day he stopped by the office to say hi. He also casually asked what I was up to that evening. My knees felt a little weak. I told him I was going to a Bikram yoga class, a practice I'd recently started. I liked it because it was so sweaty and intense it actually made me forget about my problems for an hour. "Can I come?" he asked with a grin. He said he'd never done yoga before but would be willing to try. He showed up at the appointed time outside the studio and rented a stinky communal yoga mat for the class. As we got settled, the heat rose. I felt sweat dripping down my back and class hadn't even started yet. We were both lying on our backs when he turned toward me, catching me eyeing his muscular biceps.

"So, how old are you?" he asked. I told him I was twenty-six. He grinned. I got worried. Did he think we were on a date? *Were* we on a date? "I'm way too old for you!" I whispered with a laugh. He whispered back that he didn't care. I launched into the class, running through the same twenty-six postures I'd been doing for weeks. Beside me, Logan struggled valiantly through his first class, sweat pooling under him. I was impressed. And I was definitely interested.

He showed up at my office again a week later and left a bouquet of yellow flowers for me with a note. That evening at my boss's house I asked her if she thought he liked me. She laughed incredulously.

"Libby," she said. "Are you kidding? Yellow is the perfect, respectful color. Yellow means he wants to start out as friends, when you get pink that means he really likes you, and when he gives you red, he loves you!"

BEFORE LOGAN AND I STARTED SERIOUSLY DATING, I ALSO continued to see Enrique, who had never really left the picture. He would invite me over to his house to watch TV, which was something I was free to do now that I wasn't in the church. I was also free to wear short shorts, which I did deliberately when I went over there. I knew it wasn't a good idea, any of it. Even though he had broken up with his girlfriend, I knew he wasn't the type of guy who'd be good relationship material. But I couldn't quite tear myself away, for one very basic reason: I couldn't get enough of the kissing.

We were making out on the couch one evening when he pulled back and looked at me.

"You can't have any feelings about this," he told me.

"But I like you," I said. I was confused. He said he couldn't get involved in anything serious with anyone right now. "I want to be your girlfriend," I said against all my better instincts. Mostly I just wanted to be kissing again. "Why do I even come over here?" I demanded.

"Because you can't resist me!" I laughed and kissed him again. He played a lot of games. I knew I should be just friends with him.

Finally, after I'd been out with Logan a few times, I decided I'd steer myself onto the right track and stop fooling around with Enrique. Logan treated me a lot better. When Enrique invited me over for dinner, I went—but I didn't wear my shortest shorts anymore. He cooked steaks for dinner, and assigned me to make noodles, which I promptly screwed up by over-filling the small pot he had given me. We joked around and ate dinner, and then I jumped up from the table and gave him a hug good-bye. "I made this steak dinner for you, and now you're just going to leave?" he asked, incredulous. "Yep," I answered. I headed for the door. I felt a twinge of regret that I might never get to kiss him again, but I knew this was the right decision. I gave him a big hug and left.

Months later, I got word from Megan that my family had found out about my involvement with him. "They know about that guy from the library," she told me. Apparently he'd told a judge in Lawrence about our little secret, and that guy was a friend of the family. I texted Enrique, scandalized. "A little bird told me you talked about us, and now my family knows!" I wrote. He wrote back that he didn't know what I was talking about. Same old Enrique. Mysterious, and maddening.

LOGAN WAS THE MAIN REASON I SHUT THE DOOR ON THAT part of my life. Part of me knew it was a bad idea to get involved with him, too, not only because of the age difference between us but because I had just gone through a huge, life-changing event. I was in no state to start a relationship with anyone—especially since I'd never been in one and had no idea how to navigate it. Despite knowing all of that, I said yes when he asked me to dinner.

Sitting at an Italian restaurant in Lawrence with him, I knew I had to say something about my past, and the sooner the better. It hadn't come up, and I had no idea if he knew. So I came out with it. "Do you know about my family?" I blurted out before the waiter had even brought our menus. Even though I had never been in a relationship, I knew it wasn't a good idea to start a potential one with secrets. He said he didn't, and that he didn't care about where I came from—he just wanted to get to know me.

That night, however, he Googled me. And, as he told me when we talked the next day, he was indeed shocked and disturbed at what he had found online. I had seen this coming, and I still felt sick. I told him he could call it quits if he wanted to, and lied that it wouldn't hurt my feelings at all. If I was good at one thing, it was keeping a positive face on no matter what was happening inside. But Logan said he didn't want to stop seeing me. He said he respected me for leaving and that he liked me for me. He persisted, taking me to movies, making me mix CDs, and bringing me more flowers. I began to fall in love, something I had grown up thinking I would never be allowed to do.

Without the church's disapproval looming over everything I said and did, I was free to question some of my long-held beliefs. But it's hard to jettison everything you grew up with overnight. My friendship with Blake, my volleyball buddy, had started when I was still in the church. In the early days after I'd left, he asked me what I thought about gay people now that I wasn't required to picket them anymore. "I still think it's wrong," I told him. He looked sad, stared at the ground, and changed the subject. We left it at that for months, but continued on with our volleyball games and Starbucks runs. He had become one of my closest friends, despite the fact that I knew he was gay and he knew I knew. *Why, exactly, is it so wrong?* I asked myself frequently in the weeks and months that followed. Was it really my place to judge whether someone's life was right or wrong? All my life I had been instructed to think they were awful, terrible people—but the more I thought about it, the less I could think of any examples of that being true. And here was an example of someone I loved, who didn't think he could talk to me about it because I'd be judging him.

Once, I was having a particularly hard day after having a terrible conversation with my sister, who I just learned had recently left the church. I called Blake and asked if we could meet up. He picked me up and we drove to Starbucks, with me sobbing in the passenger seat. As we parked, I turned to him.

"Blake," I blurted out, "I know you're gay. Would you just tell me? I don't care. I just want to know."

"Are you really sure you don't care?" he asked, avoiding my eyes.

"Yes!" I said with a weepy laugh. "I've never really cared. You've always treated me so well. I don't think I've ever really cared."

Slowly he nodded. "Yes," he said. "I am. I just didn't want you to hate me."

"I knew it!" I yelled. "And I don't hate you!" We hugged and I pulled a Kleenex out of my pocket and blew my nose. "Do I look like I've been crying?" I asked, feeling like my eyes were nearly swollen shut by that point from weeping.

"Uh," he said. "No?" We laughed together—a genuine, cleansing laugh. Then we got out and went to get Frappuccinos.

A FEW MONTHS AFTER LEAVING, I MANAGED TO GET MY finances in order enough to buy a house. I furnished it with items purchased at garage sales and clearance items from a local furniture store—and, of course, my beloved birthday present can opener. Logan was at the center of my life, helping me move and with any other thing I asked of him. I had a place to live now, and a boyfriend. I was really doing it—living in the world like a grownup. But I still felt like an imposter. Every day I discovered new experiences that made me feel like I was reliving my adolescence, just learning how to operate in the world.

One of the most traumatic was going to church—regular church. The first time, it was a Catholic church, in the small town where Logan grew up, Eudora. I went with Logan at his mother's insistence. It was Easter, and we had been dating for a little under a year. He comes from a somewhat religious family, so it was important to him to bring me there. Even though he wasn't too religious by that point in his life. The church had been a cornerstone of his life growing up. I respected that about him—it was something we shared, in a way—and yet the thought of going to church anywhere at all made me feel sick to my stomach. "Let's just go," he cajoled gently. "We'll sit at the back." I decided I'd suck it up, for him, and give it a try.

Midway through the service, Logan got up to get in line to take Communion, leaving me sitting in the pew with a few of his family members. I felt a mild panic attack coming on. Somehow, I thought, Gramps knew I was doing this. Sitting in a false church with a bunch of sinners. He could never forgive me now. And God could see me. There was no way I could get out of going to hell. I began to sweat uncontrollably.

Thankfully, Logan's brother Vince farted. Silent but deadly. We all knew it was him, and it was awful, and I made a face, sliding out of the pew and darting out the door. I'll always be grateful to Vince for that conveniently timed flatulence. I stood outside on the church steps, fuming, angry at Logan for putting me in this situation in the first place. How could he have been so thoughtless? Leaving me sitting there by myself!

He knew what I'd been through! Logically I knew he hadn't meant anything like that, and that I was being irrational. But logic didn't have anything to do with this.

Wiping away tears, I stormed off to a park down the road. I just wanted to get away. Actually, I wanted to go get a doughnut at Casey's General Store. I wanted comfort food, something sugary, something that would remind me of the Little Debbie snacks we used to have during church intermission, in Gran's kitchen. I would never be able to go to Gran's kitchen again. The thought made me cry harder as I sat on a park bench.

Logan had followed me out of the church and sat down next to me. He asked why I was so upset, and I was completely unable to explain. It was an instinctive reaction, almost impossible to put into words. He sat quietly holding my hand, and finally I managed to explain that I just didn't want to be pushed into going to church before I was ready. He seemed to understand, but there were more challenges to come that afternoon.

After church, we were expected to go to Logan's grandmother's house for an Easter brunch. Again, I really didn't want to go. I had already violated one of my family's taboos by going to a Catholic church, now I was expected to violate another by celebrating a pagan holiday. At lunch, the family all prayed and held hands beforehand. I was as uncomfortable as I had expected; their prayer was incredibly watered down compared to Westboro's style.

THE SECOND TIME I WENT TO A CATHOLIC CHURCH WAS FOR Logan's cousin's wedding. The part of the ceremony that most jarred me then was when you were supposed to shake hands with your neighbors. I felt as if I was being forced to be more a part of the church than I'd wanted, though I reluctantly participated. I felt I was being sucked into the Catholic religion, and I wanted no part of it. I left the building and quietly sat outside waiting for the wedding party to make their exit. Shortly after I walked out, Logan's mom emerged.

"Is everything all right? Why did you leave?" she asked.

I pushed back tears. "I feel like you're trying to push your religion onto me," I blurted. "I can't get over the whole pedophile priest scandal. I know by going in there it looks like I'm supporting it and I'm not. I just can't do it." I had shocked myself by saying that. I'd tried my hardest to steer away from any religious talk with anyone, but there was no escaping it here.

"Well, you know, by saying that, you're judging," she told me. "Not all of the priests did it, and you can't judge them based on the actions of some."

I stood my ground. "It's fact," I said. "All the news reports, all the lawsuits . . . it's not right. I don't approve of it and I'm not going to pretend it didn't happen. I do not want to go to a Catholic church. Plus all the money received in any Catholic church is fungible, so I feel like everyone is supporting pedophiles, which is wrong."

The wedding party started coming out and I got up quickly, trying to find Logan. I was shaken by what I'd said, but also proud I'd stood up for myself.

That spring, my friend Julie planned to baptize her baby—a practice I had been brought up to believe was sacrilegious. I longed to skip it, but I also didn't want to offend her by saying I wouldn't go. During the service, they received Communion, and that put me over the edge—I walked out while everyone else was lining up for the altar. The priest said something about "those who eat or drink unworthily," and I figured I wasn't worthy enough, so it seemed like a good opportunity to leave.

Afterward, we all went to lunch. My friend's mother-in-law raised an eyebrow at me. "If you hadn't left," she said, "you could have gotten your picture taken with everyone else." She seemed mad at me. For someone who had just been to a church where you were supposed to have so much compassion for your fellow humans, she didn't seem very compassionate. I tried to get away from her and sit by Julie, or our friend Lori, who both have always been understanding and compassionate, but she made it a priority to sit next to me, which made for an uncomfortable lunch.

THAT NIGHT, I THOUGHT ABOUT MY VISCERAL REACTION TO being in church. How exclusionary it had felt to me; that some churchgoers were more worthy than others. How, if you didn't take Communion, you weren't as close to God as if you had. How, historically, their priests had been shielded from punishment and prosecution when they'd preyed on children and young men.

All my experiences after leaving Westboro had left me feeling that organized religion embodied a holier-than-thou, nose-in-the-air mentality. It wasn't so noticeable outside of a church setting, but once inside the church doors, or if religion was brought up, whomever you talked to, they thought their religion was head and shoulders above the rest. And I couldn't stand it. No one, and no religion, is better than others, I thought; I just wanted to tell them to get over themselves and be nice to one another. It seemed mean and uncomfortable and unnecessary to create an aura of superiority. It seemed to me that Westboro had, in a weird way, at least been more egalitarian in their condemnation of everyone to whom they preached.

ONE AUGUST DAY IN 2010, LOGAN ASKED ME IF I WANTED TO go on a walk on a trail near my house with him, one of my favorite pastimes. I had a funny feeling he was going to ask me to marry him. I knew it was coming, because we'd gone ring shopping weeks earlier. But I still wanted the surprise of having him ask me. We went on our walk and nothing happened, and I found myself a little disappointed. I told myself to be patient and that he probably needed a little more time. As we walked in the door of my house, I saw a chair sitting in the middle of the entryway with a ring box on it—he'd secretly arranged it all on the pretense of having forgotten his sunglasses when we first started out on our walk. I was genuinely surprised—he'd pulled it off. He opened the box, got down on one knee, and asked me to marry him. With tears in my eyes, I said yes— then asked if he was sure. Who would want to marry me, with all the baggage I brought? He assured me he had made up his mind completely, then took my right hand in both of his and started to put the ring on it. Laughing, I told him he was holding the wrong hand. We were both shaky and smiling and crying a little. It was perfect.

We decided to get married on the beach in Mexico. I've always loved to travel to exotic beaches, and Logan is half Mexican, so it seemed like the ideal plan. Cozumel caught my eye as I searched for resorts that held weddings, and that quickly became our destination.

As soon as we began to make up the guest list, I had to fight back feelings of guilt and anguish at not being able to tell my family I was getting married—let alone invite them to be there on the day. I did invite some of my cousins who'd left, though: my cousins Josh, Tim, and Hez, and their significant others. Josh's wife Stephanie agreed to be one of my bridesmaids. The rest of the guests would be Logan's family and our friends.

We got to the Iberostar resort a few days early, to take care of legal paperwork and make sure all the arrangements were made. We also took a couple of excursions with friends who came down early—taking an ATV through muddy trails, nature walks that let us see and even touch wildlife and strange jungle plants. Our hike leader showed us one small, green flower that would recoil when you touched it, then slowly open back up again. I could have stayed for hours watching that plant jump back and slowly come forward again. We swam in open water with dolphins, which lifted Logan and me out of the water on their noses while they swam. I felt like I was flying. Logan didn't fare quite so well—he wobbled and face-planted into the water while the dolphins seemed like they were giggling at him.

During the rehearsal dinner, Logan's uncle Mike walked up to me. "This is it. This is forever," he said. "Are you ready for this?" I laughed and assured him I was, but internally I was flustered. What a time to ask that! Especially of someone so prone to second-guessing, which I thought might come from living a life where all my thoughts and actions had been so heavily controlled. *Making up your own mind is a lot harder,* I thought. But I didn't have any doubt in my mind that I wanted to marry Logan Alvarez.

The day of the wedding, I woke up ready to stick to the plan I'd made. I had brought makeup and some flower hairpieces I wanted to use, but I realized I didn't really know how to use any of it. Panic momentarily set in before Logan's mom recognized my cluelessness and kindly stepped in to help. As I got dressed, I put on some rings that my mother and grandmother had given me. I wanted so much for them to be there, but I knew it was impossible. I knew, also, that they'd have wanted to be there if they had been allowed to do it—or even speak of it. Overwhelming sadness mixed with the joy and excitement of the day, and I let myself give in to tears for a minute.

We took some photos in the morning under a beachside gazebo, the perfect location for our first look. Within seconds of him seeing me in my long, white beach dress, I blurted out to Logan, "Do my boobs look all right?" He burst out laughing and assured me that I looked fine. My bridesmaids had made a big deal of positioning my cleavage perfectly, so I was glad he approved. Much of the day was spent making a wedding video with the bridesmaids, groomsmen, and guests, set to "Yeah" by Usher.

Mosquitoes descended on our beach ceremony in spite of the thick cloud of repellent the resort had sprayed beforehand. But Logan and I seemed to have lucked out; we were the only ones not getting bitten. As we stood watching the afternoon sun sink over the waves, I marveled that this was happening at all. I looked around at all the people we loved who'd made the trip down here and felt so happy. We stood near a tree that had been adorned with seashells. It was so simple and beautiful. Logan and I read our own vows; we had a sand ceremony, with pink and blue sand poured together to represent our two lives meshing. My cousins read Bible verses and explained what the sand stood for.

It had started raining right before the ceremony, but stopped as Logan and I were walking down the makeshift aisle together. Everyone told us that was good luck.

Later that night, as we were lying on the bed reflecting on the day that had flown past, I told Logan how much I missed my family and wished they were there; we had agreed not to talk about it too much because of how sad it made me, but he understood, saying nothing and embracing me in one of his bear hugs. We fell asleep quickly, and I realized how right everyone was about the wedding night not actually being all that romantic. Besides, this wasn't the first time Logan and I had slept together—another way I knew I'd really burned my bridges with the church.

The day after the wedding, we took underwater ocean photos. I had heard of the tradition of brides "trashing the dress" after the wedding, which had given me the idea of jumping into the water in mine. The photographer wanted us to kiss underwater, but I found myself completely unable to do anything but blow bubbles. Finally, we figured out that if we jumped in while kissing we could get the shot.

We went across the ocean to Playa del Carmen for our honeymoon. It brought up a lot of the fears that had been drilled into me as a church member, compounded with the collective fear of the authorities cracking down on us for our views was the terror of impressionable youngsters (like me) being exposed to so many people with different views and lifestyles. The long-instilled paranoia about government crept into me every time we went through customs, where I would envision them seeing my name and then calling me into a private room to interrogate me. But nothing happened, other than one officer being short with me. We spent a glorious week, sightseeing and tasting delicious food and constantly being surprised by how welcoming everyone was. Not once did I have to stop and tell people they were going to hell.

RIGHT BEFORE LOGAN AND I LEFT FOR OUR WEDDING, I decided to tackle another first: getting my ears pierced. He thought that was funny, because it seemed so minor. But I had always thought it looked pretty, and I'd bought some dangly earrings on a whim while on vacation to Italy with Logan a year after leaving. Now, I was going to take the next step in—as the church would have said—defiling my body. My friend Bridget went with me to Claire's in Lawrence, a chain known for piercing. I went through my usual extreme nervousness and motormouthed talking, and then the woman put studs into my ears with an earring gun, and it took all of two minutes. I felt a familiar twinge of worrying that there would be spiritual repercussions to what I'd just done. But I liked the way I looked so much that I quickly put those worries aside. If I was going to hell, so was every woman I knew.

IN TOPEKA, NEAR WBC, CHANGES WERE AFOOT. IN 2012, someone bought a small ranch house across the street from Gramps's place and painted it in rainbow stripes. The rainbow, I knew from my many years of picketing, was a symbol of gay pride; we'd used it on countless signs ourselves, to mock what it stood for. I first read about the house in news stories people had posted to Facebook; I could only imagine how mad Shirl would be. I couldn't help smiling to myself about that. Gramps would probably just welcome it as more publicity for the church; my family would have said it was a good thing because it brought attention to them, and it would make a clear, visible distinction between the righteous and the unrighteous. I decided I had to go see for myself. It would be the first time I'd been in my old neighborhood since leaving.

Logan and I, plus Dana, a cousin of mine on my mom's side of the family, and her daughter, Alyssa, made the half-hour drive over to Topeka together. My stomach began twisting up as we approached the highway exit. When we turned the corner onto the street, my anxiety changed to disbelief—I forgot to think about the church for a minute while I gaped at that little house. It was one big gay pride flag of a building. I couldn't believe anyone would actually choose to paint their house like that—surely it was a promotional stunt. There was a sign on the lawn that said PLANTING PEACE and that visitors were welcome. We got out of the car and walked up the walkway. Outside, sitting in a lawn chair, was a heavyset man. I introduced myself and told him I'd grown up there, in the church across the street, and that I was nervous about being there. He took off his baseball cap and offered it to me to hide my face. It smelled awful, but I didn't want to offend him, so I thanked him and put it on. Logan and I wandered around looking at the outside of the house until two young men walked out onto the porch and introduced themselves. They didn't look like gay radicals—more like preppy college boys. One of them was Aaron Jackson, president of Planting Peace, which owned the house. The other was Davis Hammet, who worked for Aaron as the tiny charity's director of operations.

I introduced myself and told them who I was. They seemed pretty excited that I was there, especially Davis. They were busy painting the exterior, and we all offered to stick around and help.

Aaron told me they'd named this building Equality House, and that they'd bought it to deliberately make a statement to Westboro about equal rights for gay people. They wanted that little house to be a symbol for treating everyone well and decently. I loved the idea. Why wouldn't God want everyone to be treated well and decently? And who were we to say who got to go to heaven and who didn't? If Westboro was right, well, all these people would go to hell. There was nothing anyone could do to change that. And maybe, just maybe, Westboro was wrong. In that case, we would have spent our lives antagonizing people for no reason. I liked the Equality House mission better.

A week later, I went out to dinner at a Chinese restaurant with Aaron and Davis, who told me about a new project they were working on to combat bullying in schools. They wanted me to come with them to do presentations and talk about my experience of having bullied people as a picketer. That stung. I said I didn't think I had been a bully—that I had never tried to make anyone change their ways. That was God's prerogative. They pressed me on it, but nothing really came of the plan. In the process, though, we ended up having an ongoing discussion about tolerance and civil rights and religion—things I had never really talked about outside of my family. Ultimately, they both had a big influence on me being able to say, with conviction, that I don't care if someone is gay or not. Davis and I became and stayed close friends. Months later, he went with me and Blake to a drag show at KU. Afterward, Davis brought me backstage to introduce me to some of his friends who had performed and their fans. "Oh yeah, we know who you are," one of the guys said, makeup still visible around his eyes. But he said it in a friendly way, and the truth was, I'd had fun at the drag show. I didn't see what was so horrible about it, and I didn't feel the knee-jerk certainty, once second nature, that everyone involved was evil. It was definitely a new, eye-opening experience.

I found myself spending more and more time hanging out with Aaron and Davis at the Equality House. I knew my parents would have been horrified, but what did it matter now? There was a more subconscious agenda for me too, though. Standing at the front window of the house, I could look out to the front door of Gramps and Gran's house, and see any of my family members that might be passing by on their walks around the neighborhood, or to picket. Standing inside that gay pride flag–painted house was the best way for me to catch a glimpse of my family—even if it could only be a one-sided view.

One afternoon, my parents walked right by on their afternoon walk. It was the first time I had actually seen them since I'd left the church. They looked exactly the same—my dad wearing his sweatpants, my mom's long gray hair gathered into a low ponytail. I cried quietly as they walked past, completely unaware that their daughter was so close. They were right there in front of me, and yet the chasm between us was too wide for any of us to cross. "Those two walk by all the time," Aaron said. "Who are they?" "My mom and dad," I whispered through my tears. The other people in the room with me fell silent as they realized what was happening, and I just stayed at the window, staring at them until they rounded the corner and were gone.

Another afternoon while I was standing at my post near the window, Shirl came out, and then Tim, and some of Megan's teenaged brothers: Gabe, Luke, Jonah. Shirl got onto her tandem bike with Brent for a ride, and I remembered how we all used to make fun of her for buying that ridiculous thing. She started to sing. I couldn't hear it from inside the house, and I thought, if I never have to hear Shirl sing again, I'll be the happiest person alive. I wished my parents would come out again. Then I wished my parents would leave the church, so I could see them and talk to them again. I thought about how Megan and Grace had left—I had never thought Megan would leave. I thought of Anna, who'd be about eight years old by this time. I wanted her to leave. And my other nieces and nephews. I hoped they would decide to leave, too.

A DAY OR TWO BEFORE I WAS SET TO TAKE A TRIP TO NEW York in January 2013, I got a call from one of Logan's cousins. She was a little older than me and had young kids she wouldn't let me babysit, despite the fact that I offered all the time. I would have loved to have been around children again; in the church, there was no such thing as a day that you didn't spend some time with young kids. When I first met her and her family, they reminded me a little of mine, in that way. But his cousin didn't want me around—not because of my past, but because of how I had changed since leaving the church.

I was set to appear on Anderson Cooper's show during my visit, and Logan's cousin had called to give me her opinions about what I should and shouldn't say. "God has given you this platform," she said, "and you better use it to glorify Him. You know homosexuality is wrong. And you better tell people that."

"I'm not going to say that," I said, "because I don't believe that. It doesn't matter to me whether somebody is homosexual or not."

She and her family attended a very small fundamentalist church in Lawrence that shared a lot of views with Westboro. She thought I had become a questionable person because I was so accepting of people now. I had learned there were a lot of people like her out in the world, though—who basically agree with the things my former church says, but aren't brazen enough to say the things they really think in public.

When the cousin would try to talk to me about religion, she'd get really worked up; she'd cry about how much she loved God and Jesus, though she didn't seem very eager to extend a helping hand to me as I was struggling to fit into a whole new world, one where I'd given up every person I'd ever known. She would tell me that gay people "need to turn from their way and turn to Christ," and meanwhile she'd be turning her back on me.

It was the kind of behavior that reinforced my decision that I was done with religion, at least for now. I knew I would always believe in God, but that didn't have anything to do with religion for me. I could worship God however I wanted; you can do it however you want, or not, as the case may be. As long as you don't try to push yours on me, we're good. That's what we were doing in my church, I knew now: pushing our religion on others. My family would tell you differently; they'll say they are simply telling the truth. But I know better now.

How far I'd come from the days when I watched Anderson Cooper on *The Mole* and nursed a crush on him, despite suspecting that he was gay. He'd invited me to be on an episode of his show, *Anderson Live*, in which he focused on hate groups. I was used to talking to the press, so I didn't hesitate. I wanted to talk about leaving the church. Most people who knew me didn't bring it up all that often anymore, assuming I wouldn't want to reopen old wounds. It was just the opposite: I needed to open them, I needed to keep airing them out so they could heal. I was still figuring out how to think for myself, which is something you'll see if you look up the YouTube clip of that interview.

He came and talked to me a little bit before the show started; I told him that I'd had a crush on him back in the Mole days. He thought that was funny—and he told the audience about it during a commercial break! I half died of embarrassment, but had to admit it was a pretty funny story.

Right before taping, a producer took me aside and told me there was a woman in the audience whose son was a fallen soldier. Westboro had picketed his funeral, she told me, and she wanted to confront me about it. Was that OK? I panicked; nobody had warned me this would happen. But what could I say? I agreed reluctantly, and when the woman told me how much the church had hurt her and her husband, we both broke down in tears. I hadn't been at that picket; it had happened after I'd left the church. But I'd been to a hundred just like it. And I knew exactly how it had gone down.

"I'm sorry," I told her helplessly. "I thought I was doing the right thing. But I look back now and I see that we were hurting people." I couldn't bring back that woman's son, but I could maybe help her a little bit by showing her we all had the potential to change.

CHAPTER SEVEN

LIFE BEYOND WESTBORO

NEAR THE END OF 2016, I WENT TO A PROTEST AT THE KANSAS State House. There I was, in a small throng of chanting people holding signs. It all felt deeply familiar, with one glaring difference: These placards said things like LOVE TRUMPS HATE and NOT MY PRESIDENT, and, my personal favorite, YOU CAN'T COMB OVER RACISM.

At Davis's invitation, I had shown up for an anti-Trump rally. Davis was scheduled to speak, and even though only about thirty people were there, they were an enthusiastic and loud bunch. I had met some of them through Equality House events, and others seemed to know who I was already. I often still worried that strangers would yell things at me for being a Phelps, but the reaction always seemed to be that they were glad to have me around, and curious about my life after Westboro.

I took a good look at the signs people were holding, noting how paper-thin they were; the cold wind was going to make short work of them. Some had too many words crowded into a small space—I remembered Gramps saying a sign had to be pithy and get people's attention. A short sound bite to make onlookers take notice. Maybe, in the future, I could lend my sign-making abilities to this group or others like it. That was a thought that would once have been so heretical I'd have hated myself for even entertaining it.

It's been eight years since I left my family and the church, and I still feel like I'm in a constant process of adjusting to life on the outside. There is always another new experience that everyone else seems to have had decades earlier than me.

For years, it felt incredibly difficult for me to even have a normal conversation, because most of my answers pointed directly back to my upbringing—for instance, the time my now-husband's mother asked me if I worked throughout college. I said I did, and she asked where. I had worked at a law library and a law office—my family's, obviously, which made for an uncomfortable situation.

It was more than a year after I left before I finally felt comfortable just telling people who I was and where I'd come from. Before that, I always felt I'd somehow get in trouble for being who I had been, so I tried to talk around it when people asked about my family. As I'm a practicing physical therapist close to Topeka, a good percentage of my patients ask me what my maiden name is then ask if I'm related to Fred Phelps. Becoming comfortable talking about it has taken time. One day a couple of years ago, a patient asked me, as many had, if I was associated with WBC. I said, as I had done since leaving the church, that I wasn't, but that I had grown up there. Even though I was no longer a member of the church, it was difficult for me to have the conversation. But I needed to have it in order to move forward with my life. "Good," she said, "because I wouldn't want you to be my physical therapist if you were."

The year after that, I had a huge increase in patients talking about Gramps and Westboro, because my family had announced plans to picket the high school graduation in Eudora, the small town in which I worked. I had a couple of high school students as patients at the time, and they asked me if I knew who Fred Phelps was. I admitted to them he was my grandfather. They felt awkward, I'm sure—but for the first time, I didn't. I explained to them that I didn't live there anymore or practice their faith or their extracurricular activities. The mother of one of my patients would always come back and watch her son go through his exercises, and she was shocked when I told her who my grandfather was. Still, she was friendly. I could tell she didn't want to make me uncomfortable, and I felt the same way.

GRADUALLY, I'VE MADE A GOOD LIFE FOR MYSELF BEYOND Westboro. Most importantly, I have a loving husband and two wonderful children. Having kids with Logan has shown me the best kind of love; the bond between all of us is amazing. I give my kids lots of hugs and kisses; I'm affectionate in a way that my parents never were with me. (I still have reservations about public displays of affection with Logan, though! I've worked up to being OK with him holding my hand in public.) I want to raise my kids to treat people decently and to be accepting of everyone's differences. Nobody should be ashamed of how they live their life. Nobody should live in fear. Rather, they should be supported, accepted, and respected. I want my kids to be accepting of others regardless of any differences, including race, religion, or sexual orientation. I want them to see that classmate crying at school and stick up for him or her. I want my children to be happy, and to make others happy by how they treat them. I want them to have the confidence to stand up to bullies, at school and in life. I have to lead by example, of course, and I can only hope I'm doing a good job of teaching them how to treat people well.

ON JUNE 12, 2016, THE ORLANDO PULSE NIGHTCLUB MASSACRE happened. One of my first horrified thoughts, upon hearing the news, was about how the WBC members must be reacting. I knew exactly what the mood would be—celebratory. Dancing a little jig. I felt sick. How could I ever allow myself to be anything but sad, astonished and just plain disgusted by this despicable act? How had I spent so many years thinking I was doing God's work by acting jubilant when innocents were killed?

The Monday after the massacre, I took my son, Paxton, with me to a community workout group I'd joined not long before, and we had a moment of silence for the victims at the beginning of the hour. Those were two things I would have never done in my previous life: gather with others from my community, and stop to think about those killed and injured—in terms other than that they deserved it, that God was punishing them and America for their acceptance of homosexuality.

A slew of emotions ran through me. I felt sad and mad and terrified for my own children. I also felt thankful that I was even able to allow myself to have these emotions and not feel bad about it, or like I was reacting inappropriately to the situation.

It's not as easy as that, of course. There are still times, at the end of the day, when it's just me and my thoughts. I still nurse doubts about what will happen to my immortal soul when I die. I'm not sure I'll ever completely get rid of those. Fortunately, I have people I can talk with about this. People who know where I'm coming from. The younger church members are leaving more and more frequently, and it seems like every year I have another cousin on the outside.

It's a funny thing about deciding to leave the church, though: You would think that we would all be brought closer together by making the leap into the outside world, by knowing we didn't want to be a part of the Westboro mindset anymore. But the opposite seems to happen, more often than not. Becoming friendly with one another on the outside happens slowly, if at all. For many years, my sister Sharon and I barely talked, though we are now becoming closer and spending more time together. My sister Sara, to whom I was so close growing up, is now more of an acquaintance. She's had a difficult time since leaving, and doesn't seem to want a closer relationship at this time, which I had to learn to respect. When she initially came to visit me after leaving, it wasn't the happy reunion I'd hoped it would be.

Sara has had a baby herself in recent years and I've reached out to her with offers of baby clothes, but overall we see the world very differently. She doesn't approve of many of the new friends I've made, like Davis and Aaron at Equality House. She initially considered me a bad influence and she even told me at one point she didn't want me around her son, which broke my heart. But our relationship is also getting better, and I'm happy when our kids are able to get together and play now and then.

When Megan and her sister Grace left the church in 2014, I assumed Megan and I would resume our friendship and pick up where we left off. Instead, we've grown apart. Or maybe we grew apart when I left, and there was never any real chance to grow back together in our new, separate lives. Maybe that's what's necessary for many of us to make our own way in the world, after having been raised in such a small, codependent environment for so long.

MEGAN AND I WERE BRIEFLY BROUGHT CLOSE BY SOME SAD news. A little over two weeks after my firstborn, Paxton, came into the world, my grandfather died on March 19, 2014. My phone buzzed with a text from my cousin Josh, relaying the news, as I sat in the pediatrician's office with my infant in my arms.

I had known he would pass someday soon, because he'd been in hospice care for weeks. But it still came as a shock. I tried my hardest to hold back the tears as I waited for the doctor to come in. Still trying to not show emotion, like I'd always been taught. But when he came into the examination room, I fell apart. I turned to the doctor and said, "I'm crying." Obviously, because there were tears running down my cheeks. He asked me why. I told him it was because I just learned my grandpa had died. He said I had every right to cry. I told him I was upset because I didn't get to see him before he died. I apologized for crying and turned my attention to Paxton—a happy distraction. After discussing the baby for a few minutes, the doctor looked at me with sad eyes and said he was sorry about my loss. I said thank you.

When I got back to my car, I immediately called Megan. We both started crying. I thanked her for visiting Gramps, and for talking about me to him. She had gone to see him two days after Paxton was born, and I couldn't join her because I was too physically exhausted. She brought her iPhone in and recorded their conversation for me. She told him I'd had a baby, and showed him a photo. He said, "I remember her as a sweet little baby. Just a little baby. And now she's a mother." This is a quote I will forever cherish, and it's the way I want to remember him.

That was the last time Megan saw Gramps. After the family had found out she had visited him, they informed the nurses that no one was to be allowed in without my aunt Lizz's permission. As usual, they were capable of being so casually cruel—even to the person who was responsible for the church's very existence.

From what I had heard from Megan and others, it seems very likely that Gramps had dementia in the final days and weeks before he died—maybe longer. Because I wasn't able to see him, I don't exactly know how that affected him. But I wonder if perhaps it gave him a window into a different perspective. I heard that in his last days he told one of my cousins that he thought the Equality House folks were good people. Was it the dementia talking? Was it his normal Southern hospitality coming through? Or was he having a change of heart? I'll never know.

I loved Gramps. He was always kind to me. He was the first person I was close to who passed away. His death made me think more intently about the church and how it molded me growing up. I thought about how the world saw him—the only way it could have seen him—and I wished that I could show everyone the side of him that I knew, the kind and gentle side. The outside world saw Gramps as a vicious, vile, mean-tempered maniac, and I can understand why. His expressions that journalists would capture—glaring out from under his cowboy hat with his furrowed brow, and his deeply set eyes, coupled with the ruthless comments and endless Bible quotes—it all made him the perfect hate-speech icon in an era where gay civil rights were part of America's daily debate. But he was also incredibly smart and could come up with the best one-liners to grab people's attention—he really knew how to get his point across. Those were qualities that the gay community tried for in their own protests. If Gramps had only been on the other side of the issues, as he'd been when he was a civil rights lawyer. Think of what good he could have done for equality!

I know very few people will be able to see him like I did, or wonder about his potential, and I've mostly given up trying to explain myself. But I continue to believe that he meant it when he said he thought he was doing the right thing by terrorizing people on the streets day in and day out. He came from a bygone era, the Jonathan Edwards school of religion, where you showed your love for your neighbor by telling them the truth of God's word as you understood it.

The most common question that protestors would ask us, and Gramps himself, was, "How can you possibly attack these people and consider yourself a man of God? What have they ever done to you?" Time and again, he would tell them, "I'm the only one that loves you, because I'm telling you the truth. Your never-dying soul depends on this." I can't possibly defend what he did, and I know that he hurt countless people with his actions and the actions of his church, but I still believe that he saw himself as a righteous crusader, and that he loved his family. Even as I work to undo the legacy of hate that Westboro created, I hold a place in my heart for Gramps. I don't expect anyone to understand it or to sympathize, but that's *my* truth.

I HEARD, DAYS LATER, THAT WESTBORO LEADERS PUBLICLY thanked God for Gramps's death. I wasn't surprised. It seems to have moved into a more and more extreme position than even the days when I was a young adult there. Much of Shirl's power has been taken from her—which makes me wonder whether she, too, has undergone any change of heart. Davis told me that he texted Shirl that he was sorry for her loss when Gramps died. He was shocked when she texted back, "Thank you."

From what I've heard from people who have left, Steve Drain is trying to take over the leadership of the church—a shocking discovery that I learned from my cousins. Who in their right mind would let this egotistical, power-hungry tyrant take control over anything? Under his reign, the church is becoming more and more controlling, especially regarding women. The men are almost exclusively the ones allowed to appear in the media, and have declared themselves "elders," so only they can make the rules. Women aren't allow to wear shorts anymore unless they go down to the knees. Shirts have to be high; swimming suits have to be wetsuits. I can only imagine how furious Shirl is about being sidelined this way. I feel bad for her, in a way; I definitely feel bad for the other women in the church, especially my mom.

MY COUSINS JOSH AND TIMMY LEFT THE CHURCH A LITTLE over a year before I did. They wrote me a letter, after I'd gone, saying they wanted to stay in contact with me because, they wrote, I was "awesome." I was proud to get that letter. They both seem to have been able to make the transition to regular life more quickly and more easily than I did, and we've kept in pretty close touch.

Other cousins have left in recent months: twenty-three-year-old Lydia, Becky's daughter, left in 2015 and went to stay with Joe and his wife, Michelle, in Topeka. From what I've heared from her in the few conversations we've had, she seems to be adjusting to normal life really well. Another cousin, Danielle, left a year earlier. She recently joined the Marines, something Westboro would definitely not approve of.

I DON'T THINK TWICE ABOUT PEOPLE BEING GAY ANYMORE. One of my best friends is gay—Blake, who was my friend even when I was in the church. Transgender people will reach out to me on social media and I'll write back to them. I don't care what anyone is, really. If you were born a woman and you want to be a man, that's what I'll call you. If my friend Chantelle wants to be called Chaun, that's what I'll do. Because that's what makes him feel comfortable. My feelings toward gay people and transgender people are the same as toward a straight person or any other person. If they're good people, and kind, then I would love to talk to them and be friends with them. Classifications don't mean anything to me anymore. No one is better than anyone else.

If I could talk to my younger self, I would tell her to be more accepting of people, and to try to understand where they're coming from. Everybody isn't the same, and they're not going to think the same, and that's OK. WBC wants everyone to be exactly the same, to conform to their cookie-cutter version of what's acceptable, of what they say God allows. I would also tell her to listen to the inner voice telling her it's not OK to laugh at other people's misery, even when your family is instructing you to do exactly that.

SOMETIMES I SEE TRACES OF GRAMPS IN MY OWN BEHAVIOR. My husband is the most easygoing guy; he's always supportive of me and has my back. But sometimes I'll get into a state where I want to have an argument. And he won't do it. "Why won't you argue with me?" I'll yell. I feel like Gramps at those times. I definitely have a strong personality.

When I get mad at Paxton after a long day of his not listening to me—or when he's about to do something that might hurt his baby sister, Zea—I'll raise my voice, and the look on his face always makes me sad. He looks like he's trying to figure out how he's supposed to react to me, and reminds me of my own experience as a child, trying to figure out my family's irrational reactions and what I was supposed to do to please them. It definitely makes me stop and think before I raise my voice any more.

Often, when I feel my patience running thin, I think of Gran and my mom and I'm able to chill out. I also remind myself of the high expectations placed on me growing up, ones that Logan didn't have, so I have to recognize that and not get so worked up.

I still miss Gran and remember all the love she gave me and my siblings and cousins. When I watch *The Sound of Music* or *The King and I* with Paxton and Zea, I think of Gran—I was so happy to share these movies with my kids the way she shared them with me. We sing along with the songs, and I remember what a great singing voice Gran had.

I miss my parents dearly. Every night before bed I'm reminded of my mom. Zea raises her baby finger to her mouth so I'll put chapstick on her lips, and she rubs her precious hands together so I'll put lotion on her hands—just like my mom and I did when I was young. I'm reminded of my dad when Paxton grabs a ball and wants to play catch, or when he wants to go for a run around the block with me. I cherish these memories I had with my family and love the sense of comfort I get with sharing similar memories with my children.

TODAY, I FEEL MOSTLY TURNED OFF BY RELIGION AS A whole. I think I'll always believe in God, but I don't want anyone telling me how and where I can worship. Everyone should be able to have their own beliefs without being told what to think. For so many years, I pushed my religion on others. I realize this now, even though at the time, we were assured by our parents and the rest of the grownups that we weren't doing this at all, that we were simply telling people the inarguable truth.

I wonder how much longer Westboro Baptist can survive, with the rate of defections consistently going up. I believe by the time I'm old and gray, it may not be around anymore. But there are still some in my generation who are strong believers in WBC theology, so who knows—it could hang on for decades longer. Either way, I don't think it will ever have the traction it once did. The world has gotten wise to the sensationalism inherent in our picketing, and nobody seems to be very interested in paying it any attention anymore. Besides, there are so many other, more extreme outlets for hate speech these days—many of them affiliated with President Trump—that WBC seems like an old-timey relic in comparison. But I know we did our part to create an atmosphere of hate speech in this country for many years; if I could go back and change that somehow, I would.

These days, Logan and I are in the process of looking for a new home—one that will have enough extra room so that anyone who leaves the church and doesn't have a place to go can come to us. We've housed relatives who've left the church before—Megan and Danielle both spent time sleeping on our couch and moved their stuff into our storage space for a while—but I want to have a place where someone could feel comfortable staying for a bit. I never really felt like that when I left, and I now realize how valuable it is in the process of making the transition out of the church. When I left, I felt like I was a burden on the people I stayed with—and I want to help others avoid feeling that way.

I still hope I can reunite with my parents one day, so they can meet my husband and their sweet grandchildren. There are already so many years they've missed out on.

I plan to tell my kids about my past, once they're old enough to understand; this is part of why I'm writing this book. They deserve to know, and I'm sure, like all children, they'll be curious. I'll tell them that my family believed it was their duty to preach God's hatred, but that I want them to be loving and accepting of others. I'll tell them that there are lots of religions, and that if they want to be exposed to them, that's great. It's nice to get an understanding of different viewpoints—but ultimately, what I want most is for them to treat all people equally, and with kindness and dignity.

ACKNOWLEDGMENTS

I GRACIOUSLY AND SINCERELY WANT TO THANK EVERYONE who has helped me on my journey since the day I left. Megan, Faith, Brandon, Carolyn—couldn't have gotten through my initial days away from the church without you.

My family, both out of and still in the church. I wouldn't be the person I am today without going through all that life has thrown at me.

My friends Elizabeth, Brandy, Tiffany, Michelle, Adam, and Vicki, thank you for encouraging me to keep writing and for proofing and for believing in me. You guys are the best! Cheryl, Blake, Bridget, Lori, Julie, and Kristi who showed me how "normal people" act in social situations—being a little less awkward each outing is progress.

Christie May and Errin Bond for letting me share your amazing photos!

My friends at the Equality House and the NoH8 campaign, you are great examples of upstanding citizens. Your fight for basic human rights is admirable and something I am proud to support.

Thank you Sara for helping me put my thoughts together and making this something that I'm proud of—a project that can impact the lives of others! Through our many conversations, you allowed me to open up and heal and gave me the confidence in knowing I can make a difference and that my story does matter.

Finally, and most importantly, I want to thank my new family. I especially want to show gratitude to my husband, Logan, who allowed me to take time away from family to work on this project. He lovingly cared for our precious Paxton and sweet Zea and always had a hot meal on the table for us. Thank you Paxton for always laughing and dancing and brightening up my day through stressful times. Thank you Zea for always smiling and pleasantly trotting towards me on your little dainty feet, gently saying "hi" when I enter a room . . . and for being such a good sleeper so I can get things accomplished. I love you guys!

—Libby Phelps

THANKS TO IAN SPIEGELMAN, FOR YOUR COWRITING COUNSEL and for connecting Libby and me with our lovely agent, Markus Hoffmann; Markus, for being so supportive and patient with our lengthy writing process; Margi Conklin, my *New York Post* editor at the time, who trusted me to chase a story in Kansas about a girl who made a unique left turn in life; Alexandra and Brianna at Skyhorse for shepherding our manuscript through the editing and publication process; and my husband Todd, for being a reliable source of good advice, bad jokes, and general awesomeness. Most of all thanks to Libby, for inviting me into your home and your life, for sharing your story with me, and for pairing up with me to flesh it out into a book. You're a remarkable person, and I know you'll do more great things in the future.

—Sara Stewart